teach® yourself

english
vocabulary
martin hunt

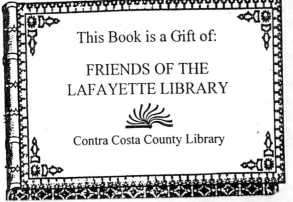
For over 60 years, more than
40 million people have learnt over
750 subjects the **teach yourself**
way, with impressive results.

u want to be
with **teach yourself**

For UK order enquiries: please contact Bookpoint Ltd, 130 Milton Park, Abingdon, Oxon OX14 4SB. Telephone: +44 (0) 1235 827720. Fax: +44 (0) 1235 400454. Lines are open 09.00–18.00, Monday to Saturday, with a 24-hour message answering service. Details about our titles and how to order are available at www.teachyourself.co.uk

For USA order enquiries: please contact McGraw-Hill Customer Services, PO Box 545, Blacklick, OH 43004-0545, USA. Telephone: 1-800-722-4726. Fax: 1-614-755-5645.

For Canada order enquiries: please contact McGraw-Hill Ryerson Ltd, 300 Water St, Whitby, Ontario L1N 9B6, Canada. Telephone: 905 430 5000. Fax: 905 430 5020.

Long renowned as the authoritative source for self-guided learning – with more than 40 million copies sold worldwide – the **teach yourself** series includes over 300 titles in the fields of languages, crafts, hobbies, business, computing and education.

British Library Cataloguing in Publication Data: a catalogue record for this title is available from the British Library.

Library of Congress Catalog Card Number: on file.

First published in UK 2001 by Hodder Arnold, 338 Euston Road, London, NW1 3BH.

First published in US 2001 by Contemporary Books, a Division of the McGraw-Hill Companies, 1 Prudential Plaza, 130 East Randolph Street, Chicago, IL 60601 USA.

This edition published 2004.

The **teach yourself** name is a registered trade mark of Hodder Headline Ltd.

Copyright © 2001, 2004 Martin Hunt

Typeset by Transet Limited, Coventry, England.
Printed in Great Britain for Hodder Arnold, a division of Hodder Headline, 338 Euston Road, London NW1 3BH, by Cox & Wyman Ltd, Reading, Berkshire.

Hodder Headline's policy is to use papers that are natural, renewable and recyclable products and made from wood grown in sustainable forests. The logging and manufacturing processes are expected to conform to the environmental regulations of the country of origin.

Impression number   10 9 8 7 6 5 4 3
Year   2009 2008 2007 2006 2005

contents

introduction

Welcome to *Teach Yourself English Vocabulary*. We want you to enjoy this book and enjoy learning English.

Why buy this book?

This book is written in English. Studying in English is the best way to remember and learn. A word in English may not be the same in your language, even though it looks the same, so it is better to know it in English. All the work you do in this book will help you have better English skills.

What is in this book?

Here you will find useful, everyday English words. You will also find extra help such as which verbs to use, and extra words to help you say more things. It explains words and gives you a chance to use them.

How to use this book

Look at the Contents (page iii) and find something that is interesting, or that you need, and study it. You decide what to do and when to do it. When you finish, try another unit that is linked. Each unit has ideas about where to go if you are not sure.

Each unit starts with **Basics**. Check you know all these words. The book will help you, but use a dictionary if you need it. When you think you know the words, try **Test your basics**. Next is **Extension**. Here, learn more words and get help with problems such as difficult verbs before trying the exercises in the next section, **Practice**. Then there is **In use** – practice exercises using the language in real situations. Finally, there is **Recap**, to help, check and remember, and write down what you have done. At the end of each unit you will also find an **Answer key** to check your work. The text of the recordings (transcripts) is at the back of the book.

British English/American English

We use square brackets to show that there are different words in British English and American English for the same idea.

For example: I like your [trousers/pants].

Trousers is British English.
Pants is American English.

For example: I [have got/have] two dogs and a cat.

I have got two dogs and a cat is British English.
I have two dogs and a cat is American English.

There are British and American voices on the recordings, so you hear both British and American pronunciation. There are very few words which are different, but where a word is *only* found in British English it is spoken by a British voice, and where a word is found *only* in American English it is spoken by an American voice. Do not worry too much about the differences – they are very small. English is English, however it is pronounced, all over the world!

Where to start?

Start with Unit 1. This will help you with words we use in the book to teach the vocabulary. Then you decide which unit to do next.

And finally ...

Good luck! We hope you enjoy the book and find it useful.

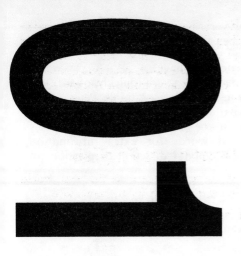

01

language to learn language

In this unit you will learn
- words to talk about language
- words to talk about learning
- how to use this book

Basics

Do you know these words? Check in a dictionary.

1	Verb	Action (go, have...)
2	Adverb *наречие*	How we do a verb (quickly, often...)
3	Noun	Thing/object/person (table, Peter...)
4	Adjective *прилаг*	What a thing/person is like (big, old...)
5	Article	A, an, the
6	Preposition	Small words for extra information, usually about direction or position (of, on ...)
7	Pronunciation	How to say a word
8	Spelling	The letters that make a word
9	Meaning	What we understand from the word

Test your basics

Cover the words above so you can't see them. Then write the English word in the space provided.

1 The letters that make a word   *spelling*
2 Small words for extra information
  (of, on...)
3 Thing/object/person (table, Peter...)
4 Action (go, have...)
5 A, an, the
6 How we do a verb (quickly, often...)
7 What a thing/person is like (big, old...)
8 What I understand from the word
9 How to say a word

Extension

More words – grammar

- When we talk about **grammar**, we talk about the rules of a language; when we talk about **vocabulary**, we talk about the words in a language.

- **Word order** is which comes first, second, third... For example:
  An old man (word order ✔) ~~old man an~~ (word order ✗)

Language of instruction

- A **question** asks you something (What's your name?).
- An **answer** gives a reply to a question (My name is Martin).
- An **exercise** is a group of questions.
- To **mark** your answers is to check which ones are correct (✔) and which are wrong (✗).

There are many types of exercises in this book:

- **Fill the gap** – put a word or words into the space
  How _old_ are you?
- **Match** – join an answer with arrows/lines
  How old are you? ⟶ Martin
  What's your name? ⟶ 20
- **Correct** – find the mistake and make it a right answer
        name
  My ~~nayme~~ is Martin
- **Choose the correct answer** – which is correct?
  How old are you?   a. 25   b. Martin   *a*

Listening

- There are also two **cassettes** or CDs with this book.
- When you **listen**, don't say anything! What can you hear?
- When you **repeat**, listen first, then say what is on the **recording**.
- Each listening exercise will have a **recording number** so you know where you are (for example, Unit 1, recording 1.1).
- A **transcript** is a written copy of the words you hear on listening.

In the classroom

- Work you do in class is called **classwork**; extra work you do at home is called **homework**.
- If you **check** your homework, you see how good it is, how many answers are correct.
- A class will usually have one **teacher** and many **students**.
- To help explain things to a class, many teachers will write on a **whiteboard** or a **blackboard**.
- If a teacher asks you to work **on your own**, then you work alone, without anyone to help.

• Teachers also often ask their students to work **in pairs**, two students together; if three or more students work together, we call this working in a **group**.

Practice

Exercise 1 Look at the words below and put them into the correct box.

go	big	a	of	quickly	table	on	Peter	often	old
have	fat	an	France	be	by	the	happily		

Verb	Adverb	Noun
go *have, be by*	*quickly often*	*table Peter France*
Adjective	**Article**	**Preposition**
big *old fat happily*	*a an the*	*on of by*

Exercise 2 Answer the questions with the correct word.

What do you call...

1 the way we say a word?   *pronunciation*

2 where words go in a sentence?   _____

3 when you say what you hear on
a recording?   _____

4 a group of questions together?   _____

Exercise 3 Find five words from this unit in the word square below.

Y	C	V	E	R	B	L
R	H	D	I	F	A	I
A	O	O	T	P	T	S
C	O	R	R	E	C	T
G	S	S	X	B	M	E
R	E	P	E	A	T	N

Now check your answers.

▶ **Exercise 4 (Recordings 1.1, 1.2, 1.3)** Pronunciation practice. Listen and repeat the words on the recording. Use the transcript at the back of the book to help you if necessary.

In use

Reading

Before you start, check you know this word: | opposite |

Readings 1 & 2 Look at the test paper below. First put in all the missing information. Then see how many of the questions you can do.

Duvall English School – Spring Test

Name   **Class**   **Teacher**

Exercise 1

Match each word to its opposite:

1 hot   young
2 old   thin
3 fat   cold

(*3 marks*)

Exercise 2

_____ the _____ !

1 He is *a* teacher.
2 _____ name's Martin. What's your name?
3 How _____ are you? 32.

(*3 marks*)

Exercise 3

_____ the mistakes.

1 I live in a ~~houses~~. *house*
2 How ar you?
3 My son is too years old.
4 My pronounciation is bad.

(*4 marks*)

Total _____ (out of 10)

▶ Listening

Before you start, check you know these words:

mistake   whiteboard

You will hear four short conversations at the Duvall School of English taken from different parts of a lesson (grammar, listening, vocabulary, etc.).

Listening 1 (Recording 1.4) Listen and put the parts of the lesson in the correct order. Be careful! One part is *not* used.

| Checking homework | *1* | Grammar | | Listening | |
| Reading | | Vocabulary | | | |

Listening 2 (Recording 1.4) Listen again and match the instruction to the part of the lesson it is taken from. One instruction and one part of the lesson are *not* used.

Part of the lesson   **Instruction**

1 Checking   a You have to match the word on the
  homework   left with its meaning on the right.

2 Grammar   b ...fill in the gaps with the missing
                        word.

3 Listening   c ...see if you can correct the sentences.

4 Reading   d Check the spelling of each word.

5 Vocabulary   e ...choose the best answer, A, B, C or D.

Now check your answers.

Recap

Here are the words we learned in this unit. Do you know them all? Write down the translations if you need to.

Language

verb	adverb	noun
adjective	article	preposition
spelling	meaning	grammar
vocabulary	word order	

Instructions

question	exercise	answer
mark	fill the gap	correct
match	listen	repeat
choose the correct answer		

Listening

cassette	CD	recording
transcript		

In the classroom

classwork	homework	check
teacher	student	whiteboard
blackboard	on your own	in pairs
group		

What to do next

- If you go to a class, listen carefully to your teacher's instructions.
- Look at any books you use. Look at the instructions.

Why not try this unit next?

- Ideas for learning vocabulary

Answer key for this unit

Test your basics

1 spelling
2 preposition
3 noun
4 verb
5 article

6 adverb
7 adjective
8 meaning
9 pronunciation

Exercise 1

Verb	Adverb	Noun
go, have, be	happily, quickly, often	table, Peter, France
Adjective	**Article**	**Preposition**
big, old, fat	a, an, the	of, on, by

Exercise 2

1 pronunciation
2 word order
3 repeat
4 exercise

Exercise 3

Y	C	V	E	R	B	L
R	H	D	I	F	A	I
A	O	O	T	P	T	S
C	O	R	R	E	C	T
G	S	S	X	B	M	E
R	E	P	E	A	T	N

Reading

Readings 1 & 2

Duvall English School – Spring Test

Name   **Class**   **Teacher**

Exercise 1

Match each word to its opposite:

1 hot   young
2 old   thin
3 fat   cold

(*3 marks*)

Exercise 2

Fill the *gaps* !

1 He is *a* teacher.
2 *My* name's Martin. What's your name?
3 How *old* are you? 32.

(*3 marks*)

Exercise 3

Correct the mistakes.

1 I live in a ~~houses~~.   *house*
2 How ~~ar~~ you?   How *are* you?
3 My son is too years old.   My son is *two* years old.
4 My pronounciation is bad.   I have bad *pronunciation*.

(*4 marks*)

Total _____ (out of 10)

Listening

Listening 1

| Checking homework | 1 | Grammar | 3 | Listening | 4 |
| ~~Reading~~ | | Vocabulary | 2 | | |

Listening 2

Part of the lesson   **Instruction**

1 Checking homework   …see if you can correct the sentences. (c)

2 Grammar   …choose the best answer, A, B, C or D. (e)

3 Listening   …fill in the gaps with the missing word. (b)

4 ~~Reading~~   ~~Check the spelling of each word~~. (d)

5 Vocabulary   You have to match the word on the left with its meaning on the right. (a)

02

ideas for learning language

In this unit you will learn
- words for learning language
- ways of improving your English
- how to ask for help with your learning

Basics

Do you know these words? Check in a dictionary and write the word in your language in the space provided. *ссли, при угнол*

1 dictionary

A book which gives the meaning of words

_____

2 pen

_____

3 notebook

_____

4 cassette (tape) recorder

_____

5 cassette (tape)

_____

6 CD player

_____

7 CD

_____

8 television

_____

9  [video recorder/ VCR]

_____

10  computer

_____

11 textbook

A book with information used in schools and colleges

_____

Test your basics

Cover the words on page 12 so you can't see them. Then write the English word in the space provided.

1

CD player

_____

7

_____

2

_____

8

_____

3

_____

9 A book which gives the
meaning of words

_____

4
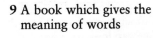

_____

10

_____

5

_____

11 A book with information
used in schools and
colleges

_____

6

_____

Extension

Verbs

- We **read** a book but an author **writes** a book.
- We can **listen** to someone else or we can **speak** ourselves.
- To **write something down** is to record information, for example new words or vocabulary.
- If you don't know something, you can **ask** a question for another person to **answer**. For example:

Question	Answer
Where does Mika come from?	☹ I'm sorry, I don't know. ☺ He comes from Sweden.

- Sometimes we must **search** for information.
- We can **look up** a word in a dictionary – that is find that word in a dictionary.
- We can **find out** information – that is look in many places to find what we need; find out is more general than look up. For example:
    Look up the word 'vocabulary' in your dictionary.
    Find out everything you can about France.

Sources

You can find English in lots of places. You can:
- **Listen** to the radio; listen to a **song** in English or buy one on CD.
- We **watch** television or **watch** a [film/movie]; we can also **see** a [film/movie].
- If you have a **computer** with an **internet** connection you can **surf** the **internet** or you can **use a CD-ROM** which might have lots of information (for example, a dictionary on a CD-ROM).
- You can **work** with a computer or a textbook to help you with your English.
- You can also read **books**, **magazines**, and **newspapers**.
- You can use a [video recorder/VCR] to **record** something that's on television so you can watch it later; you can also **record** something on a tape recorder.
- If something is difficult, you can [**practise/practice**], that is, do it again and again. You can **do** an **exercise**, for example, from a textbook, to help you.

Questions

If you need something that somebody else has …

- **Have you got...?/Do you have...?** Yes, I have./No, I haven't.
- **May I borrow...?** or **May I use...?** Yes, of course./No, I'm sorry, I'm using it. No, I'm sorry, I need it myself.

To ask to use something:
- **May I watch television?**
- **May I listen to the radio?**
- **May I use the computer?**
- **May I surf the internet?**

Practice

Exercise 1 Here are some anagrams of things you can use to help you learn a foreign language. Put the letters in the correct order to make a word. For example:

koboeton   *notebook*

1 teerinnt	2 DC repaly
3 yarntidico	4 decorrer edovi
5 CO-RDM	6 neviletois
7 zaamigen	8 seexirce

Exercise 2 Verbs and objects. Match the two parts of the sentences together.

1 I like to write down new words...	**a** CD player.
2 I often use my CD-ROM dictionary...	**b** an exercise on it.
3 Why don't you record this [programme/program]...	**c** in my notebook.
4 You can play your CD on my...	**d** in a dictionary.
5 Let's look the word up...	**e** on my computer.
6 It's amazing what you find when you surf...	**f** television.
7 If I find something difficult, I like to do...	**g** the internet.
8 You can hear lots of English if you watch...	**h** on the [video/VCR]?

Exercise 3 Fill in the gaps in the sentences below with the correct English word.

1 Have you *got* a dictionary?   Yes, I have.
2 May I borrow a pen?   No, I'm sorry. I'm _____ it.
3 _____ I use the computer?   Yes, of course.
4 Do you have a CD-ROM   _____, I don't.
  dictionary?
5 May I _____ to the radio?   No, I'm sorry, I need it myself.
6 May I read your magazine?   Yes, of _____ .

Now check your answers.

▶ **Exercise 4 (Recordings 2.1, 2.2, 2.3)** Pronunciation practice. Listen and repeat the words on the recording. Use the transcript at the back of the book to help you if necessary.

In use

Reading

Before you start, check you know these words:

| easy useful |

Note: 'Your own language' is the language you speak, for example, Spanish, Japanese, French.

In **Reading 1** below, there is an introduction to a language book giving advice on how to learn English. Look at the words in the box; which words do you think will appear?

| computer | film | newspaper | |
| dictionary | internet | tape recorder | |

Reading 1 Now read the text and put a ✔ next to those words that you find.

Ideas for learning English

1 _____

Find as much English around you as you can. Read newspapers or magazines, even if you can only read a few words. See how much you can understand. Listen to the radio, watch television or see a film – hear as much English as you can, it all helps. Read books – some books are written in easy English to help you understand, especially stories. Try some of these. Newspapers and magazines are also a good source of spoken English because they have many interviews.

2 _____

If you don't know a word, you can look it up in a dictionary. You can use a dictionary that tells you English words in your own language, or try using an English–English dictionary and see how much you understand. Keep a dictionary with you when you use this book – it's very useful, but don't look in it for every word. See if you can understand first, and only look up the most important words you don't know.

3 _____

In today's world, there's nothing better than using a computer. There are some very good dictionaries on CD-ROM, with video and plenty of practice activities. If you can surf the internet, then there is almost no limit to the information out there, and most of it is in English.

4 _____

Listen carefully to how someone says an English word. See if you can hear the word on television or radio, and try to record it. Use a tape recorder to record yourself. Listen to yourself speak and then try again. In this book, you will find lots of places to listen and repeat.

Reading 2 The headings have been taken out of the text and are in the box below. Put each heading in the correct place in the text. One heading is not used.

Listening very carefully   Using a dictionary
                 Finding things out
      English is everywhere   Saying it right

▶ Listening

In **Listening 1** you will hear an interview with a student, Marc Roussell, who spent some time studying in the USA. Look at the box of words from **Reading 1** below. Which words do you think Marc will say?

computer	film	newspaper	
dictionary	internet	tape recorder	

Listening 1 (Recording 2.4) Listen and put a ✔ next to the words Marc says.

Listening 2 (Recording 2.4) Listen again and choose the correct word in the sentences below.

1 You hear the ~~radio~~/**language** all the time.
2 You know, you watch **television/a film** and it's in English.
3 I think looking in the dictionary all the time is a **good/bad** idea.
4 I looked up New York **on the internet/in a magazine**.
5 We learned **American/British** English at school.

Now check your answers.

Recap

Here are the words we learned in this unit. Do you know them all? Write down the translations if you need to.

Objects and sources

dictionary	pen	notebook
cassette (tape) recorder	cassette (tape)	CD player
	CD	song
television	[video (recorder)/VCR]	textbook
computer	CD-ROM	books
exercise	internet	magazines
newspapers		

Verbs

read	write	write down
record	listen	speak
ask	answer	search
look up	find out	do
[practise/practice]		

Questions and answers

Have you got...?	Do you have...?	Yes, I have.
No, I haven't.	May I borrow...?	May I use...?
Yes, of course.	No, I'm sorry.	May I watch TV?
May I listen to the radio?	May I use the computer?	May I surf the internet?

What to do next

- Try to watch television, see a film, or listen to the radio in English.
- Listen to songs in English.
- If you can use a computer, try to buy English CD-ROMs.
- Surf the internet – look for something you are interested in.
- Read interviews in magazines and newspapers.
- Whatever you do, try to use as much English as possible!

Which unit next?

Look at the list of units in this book; choose one you need to learn, or that looks interesting, and try it. Good luck!

Answer key for this unit

Test your basics

1

CD player

4

CD

2

computer

5

[video (recorder)/VCR]

3

television

6

cassette (tape) recorder

7

cassette (tape)

8

pen

9 A book which gives the
meaning of words

dictionary

10

notebook

11 A book with information
used in schools and
colleges

textbook

Exercise 1

1 internet
2 CD player
3 dictionary
4 video recorder
5 CD-ROM
6 television
7 magazine
8 exercise

Exercise 2

1 I like to write down new words *in my notebook.*
2 I often use my CD-ROM dictionary *on my computer.*
3 Why don't you record this [programme/program] *on the [video/VCR]?*
4 You can play your CD on my *CD player.*
5 Let's look the word up *in a dictionary.*
6 It's amazing what you find when you surf *the internet.*
7 If I find something difficult, I like to do *an exercise on it.*
8 You can hear lots of English if you watch *television.*

Exercise 3

1 Have you *got* a dictionary?   Yes, I have.
2 May I borrow a pen?   No, I'm sorry, I'm *using* it.
3 *May* I use the computer?   Yes, of course.
4 Do you have a CD-ROM   *No*, I don't.
   dictionary?
5 May I *listen* to the radio?   No, I'm sorry, I need it myself.
6 May I read your magazine?   Yes, of *course*.

Reading

Reading 1

computer	✔	film	✔	newspaper	✔
dictionary	✔	internet	✔	tape recorder	✔

(*All 6 words appear*)

Reading 2

1 English is everywhere
2 Using a dictionary
3 Finding things out
4 Saying it right

'Listening very carefully' is not used.

Listening

Listening 1

~~computer~~		~~film~~		newspaper	✔
dictionary	✔	internet	✔	~~tape recorder~~	

Listening 2

1 You hear the *language* all the time.
2 You know, you watch *television* and it's in English.
3 I think looking in the dictionary all the time is a *bad* idea.
4 I looked up New York *on the internet*.
5 We learned *British* English at school.

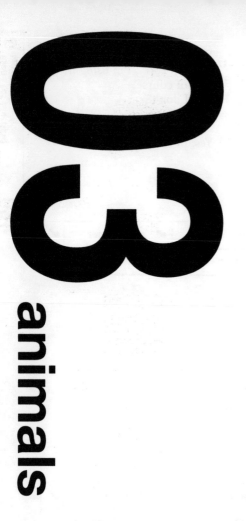

03

animals

In this unit you will learn
- the names of many animals
- parts of an animal's body
  (wing, claw...)
- how to describe animals

Basics

Do you know these words? Check in a dictionary and write the word in your language in the space provided.

1 cat

_____

2 dog

_____

3 bird

_____

4 horse

_____

5 mouse

_____

6 elephant

_____

7 insect

_____

8 cow

_____

9 fish

_____

Test your basics

Write the English word in the space provided. Don't look at page 23!

1

insect

2

mouse

3

elephang

4

dog

5

cow

6

cat

7

fish

8

houzse

9

bird

Extension

More animals

- A **lion** is a big cat that lives in the jungle; the **tiger** is another big cat with orange and black stripes.
- The **shark** lives in the sea and is very dangerous; a **snake** is also very dangerous and can be poisonous.
- A **duck** is a bird that can also swim; a **sheep** (plural **sheep**) is a farm animal while a **camel** lives in the desert.
- A **tortoise** is an animal that's very slow and can live a long time.

Birds

Nouns

- **Wings** help a bird to fly.
- A **beak** is a bird's mouth.
- Some birds have **webbed feet** to help them swim.
- Many birds don't have hair, they have **feathers**.
- Birds don't live in houses, they live in **nests**.

Verbs

- Many birds can **fly** through the air.

Fish

Nouns

- A shark has a top **fin**.
- Most fish use a **tail** to help them swim.
- Fish live in the **sea** or in **rivers** or in **lakes**.

Verbs

- Fish **swim** through water.

Land animals

Nouns

- Many animals have 'hair'; we call it **fur**; it feels very **soft**.
- Some animals like elephants have no fur, they have **skin** like we do.
- Many animals walk on four **legs**.

- Animals like dogs and cats have **paws**, not hands or feet; horses have **hooves**.
- A cat can hurt you with its sharp **claws**.
- Some animals have many **teeth**.

Verbs

- Very fast animals can **run**; very slow animals like the tortoise **crawl**.
- A cat can **scratch** you with its claws or **bite** you with its teeth.

Describing an animal

Adjectives

big	fast	dangerous	long
intelligent	wild	small	slow
friendly	short	stupid	tame

Writing sentences

A... is a(n)... animal with... and... It can... but it can't... It comes from...

Example: A *camel* is a *big* animal with *brown fur* and a *long tail*. It can *walk a long way*, but it can't *swim*. It comes from *Africa* and *hot countries*.

Practice

Exercise 1 Can you guess these animals?

1 A *tiger* has four paws, likes fish, and has a long tail.
2 A _____ has a large fin and lives in the sea. It is very dangerous.
3 A _____ is a large animal that can run very fast. It has four hooves.
4 A _____ is an animal that can fly and lives in nests.
5 A _____ is a dangerous animal that can bite you. It has no legs, but it lives on land.
6 A _____ is a very small animal. It has a long tail, big teeth, and it likes cheese!

Exercise 2 Find the ten animal parts/verbs in the word square and put the words under the correct animal.

B	E	A	K	A	S	W	V	F	B
L	Q	H	O	O	V	E	S	E	M
F	U	R	L	P	L	B	K	A	O
G	H	M	E	D	F	B	I	T	T
W	I	N	G	S	I	E	N	H	I
O	P	W	S	Z	N	D	A	E	V
H	U	L	W	B	X	F	Z	R	D
A	G	W	M	C	J	E	S	S	I
S	H	A	R	P	T	E	E	T	H
T	J	S	B	S	O	T	E	V	J

DUCK	CAMEL	SHARK
Beak		_eath_

Exercise 3 Complete these sentences with the words in the box below. Be careful – one word is not used.

1 The elephant is a *large* animal with four ___legs___ and [grey/gray] ___skin___.
2 Be careful of the cat! She might ___scratch___ you with her ___claws___.
3 I love sheep, but they're so _____. They always walk on the road in front of cars.
4 Our mouse is so ___soft___. I love his [grey/gray] ___fur___.
5 The lion ___comes___ from Africa; it is a very ___dangerous___ animal.

scratch   skin   dangerous   soft   legs
comes   ~~large~~   fur   claws   stupid   wings

Now check your answers.

▶ Exercise 4 (Recordings 3.1, 3.2, 3.3, 3.4) Pronunciation practice. Listen and repeat the words on the recording. Use the transcript at the back of the book to help you if necessary.

In use

Reading

Below are the notices for four animals in a zoo. Before you start reading, check you know these words:

> male   female   grass   enemy   give birth   hunt   egg
> kmh ([kilometres/kilometers] per hour)   dive   grow   ink   hide

Reading 1 Read the notices below and write the name of each animal under the pictures on page 29. One animal is not used.

The Hippopotamus (plural: hippopotamuses) The *hippopotamus*, or hippo for short, lives in Africa in wet places. It weighs up to 1,400kg and can live for nearly fifty years in the zoo. Male hippos generally live alone, but female hippos often live in groups of ten to fifteen. Hippos eat many types of grass and only have two enemies: other hippos and, sadly, humans.

The Cockroach *Cockroaches* are insects. They have survived for 250 million years! Cockroaches are very small, only a few [centimetres/centimeters] long. Cockroaches can live for up to two years and give birth to fifteen to forty young. Cockroaches are great survivors; they can lose their heads and live for a week, dying only because they cannot drink any water!

The Golden Eagle The *golden eagle* is a bird of prey. This is a bird that hunts for its food, eating other small animals such as rabbits and mice. The female often looks after the eggs, but sometimes the male does. Golden eagles are very fast – they fly at 50 kmh, but can dive at speeds of up to 150 kmh!

The Octopus (plural: octopuses) The *octopus* has eight legs, and it can grow new ones if they are damaged! The octopus can change [colour/color], and it can release 'ink' into the sea which helps it hide from other animals. The octopus has excellent eyes and hunts at night. And did you know the octopus also has three hearts?

Reading 2 Decide if the sentences below are true or false. Then correct the ones which are false.

Sometimes male eagles look after the young.   ✔

~~Male hippos live together in groups.~~ Female hippos live together in groups.

1 Hippos eat meat.
2 Cockroaches are big animals.
3 Cockroaches can live without their heads for seven days.
4 Eagles can only fly at 50 kmh.
5 An octopus always has eight legs.
6 Humans are a friend of the hippo.
7 Rabbits sometimes hunt eagles.
8 The octopus can be different [colours/colors].

▶ Listening

Before you start, check you know these words:

Africa	pet	silver	gold

Note: *Paddington Bear* is the name of a famous British toy bear; *goldfish* is a type of small fish.

Animal Rules is a popular quiz show on radio. It is played with two people. One person has to listen to his/her partner and guess the animal.

Listening 1 (Recording 3.5) Look at the animals below. Listen to the recording and number them in the order you hear them. Be careful! One animal is *not* used.

goldfish		bear		dog	
cat		lion	*1*	duck	

Listening 2 Listen to the recording again. Match an animal with a sentence in the box below. Be careful! One animal and one sentence are *not* used!

goldfish	It has got long claws.
cat	It's very dangerous.
bear	It has got four big paws.
lion	Lots of people have these as pets.
dog	It can swim.
duck	It has a tail.

Now check your answers.

Recap

Here are the words we learned in this unit. Do you know them all? Write down the translations if you need to.

Animals

cat	dog	bird
horse	mouse (mice)	elephant
insect	cow	fish
lion	tiger	shark
snake	duck	sheep
camel	tortoise	

Living places

nest	sea	river
lake		

Parts of animals

wings	beak	webbed feet
feathers	fin	tail
fur	skin	legs
paws	claws	teeth
hooves		

Verbs

fly	swim	run
crawl	scratch	bite

Adjectives

big	small	fast
slow	dangerous	friendly
long	short	intelligent
stupid	sharp	soft
wild	tame	

What to do next

- Try playing a game of 'animal rules' with another student.
- Think of animals in your country; describe them in English.
- Look up the names of animals in your country in an English dictionary.
- Describe your [favourite/favorite] animal in English; describe an animal you hate.
- Look at animal sites on the internet.

Why not try this unit next?

- Body (1)

Answer key for this unit *equina*

Test your basics

1 insect

2 mouse

3 elephant

4 dog

5 cow

6 cat

7 fish

8 horse

9 bird

Exercise 1

1 cat	2 shark	3 horse
4 bird	5 snake	6 mouse

Exercise 2

B	E	A	K	A	S	W	V	F	B
L	Q	H	O	O	V	E	S	E	M
F	U	R	L	P	L	B	K	A	O
G	H	M	E	D	F	B	I	T	T
W	I	N	G	S	I	E	N	H	I
O	P	W	S	Z	N	D	A	E	V
H	U	L	W	B	X	F	Z	R	D
A	G	W	M	C	J	E	S	S	I
S	H	A	R	P	T	E	E	T	H
T	J	S	B	S	O	T	E	V	J

DUCK	CAMEL	SHARK
beak	legs	fin
wings	hooves	skin
webbed feet	fur	sharp teeth
feathers		

Exercise 3

1 The elephant is a *large* animal with four *legs* and [grey/gray] *skin*.
2 Be careful of the cat! She might *scratch* you with her *claws*!
3 I love sheep but they're so *stupid*! They always walk on the road in front of cars!
4 Our mouse is so *soft*. I love his [grey/gray] *fur*.
5 The lion *comes* from Africa; it is a very *dangerous* animal!

Reading

Reading 1

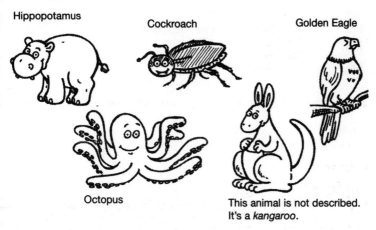

Hippopotamus

Cockroach

Golden Eagle

Octopus

This animal is not described. It's a *kangaroo*.

Reading 2

1 ~~Hippos eat meat~~.   Hippos eat grasses.
2 ~~Cockroaches are big animals~~.   Cockroaches are small animals.
3 Cockroaches can live without their heads for seven days.   ✔

4 ~~Eagles can only fly at 50 kmh.~~   Eagles can dive at up to 150 kmh.
5 An octopus always has eight legs.   ✔
6 ~~Humans are a friend of the hippo.~~   Humans are an enemy of the hippo.
7 ~~Rabbits sometimes hunt eagles.~~ Eagles sometimes hunt rabbits.
8 The octopus can be different colours.   ✔

Listening

Listening 1

goldfish	3	bear	2	dog	✘
cat	5	lion	1	duck	4

Listening 2

goldfish	Lots of people have these as pets.
cat	It has a tail.
bear	It has got four big paws.
lion	It's very dangerous.
duck	It can swim.

('dog' and 'It has got long claws' are not used)

04

body (1)

In this unit you will learn
- parts of the face and the head
- words for colour, age, hair style
- how to ask questions about/describe a face

Basics

Do you know these words? Check in a dictionary and write the word in your language.

HEAD

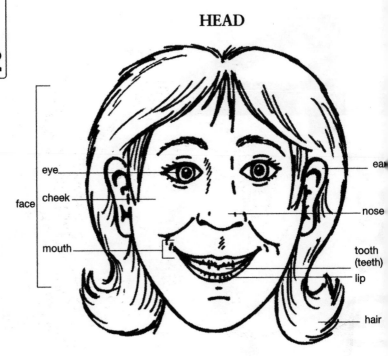

eye

cheek

face

mouth

ear

nose

tooth
(teeth)

lip

hair

Test your basics

Cover the words on page 26. Then write the English word in the space below.

1 *head*

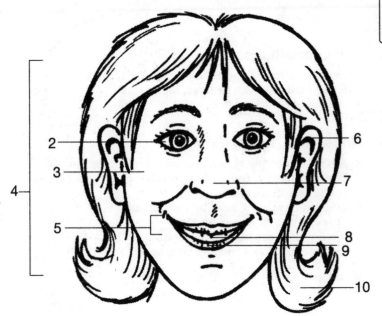

Extension

Hair

- Length: hair can be **long** or **short**.
- Thickness: hair can be **thick** or it can be **thin**. If you have no hair, you are **bald**.
- [Colour/color]: hair can be **fair**, **dark**, **blond**, **brown**, **black**, [**grey/gray**], **white** or **red**.
- Style: hair can be **straight**, **wavy** or **curly**.
- A man can have a **beard** or a **moustache**, but most men are **clean-shaven**.

Eyes, mouth, lips

- Eye [colour/color]: **green**, **blue**, [**grey/gray**], **brown**.
- Eyes and mouth can be **large**, **big** or **small**.
- **Lips** can be **thick** or **thin**.

Nose, face, head, ears

- A nose can be **big** or **small**. It can also be **long** and **thin**.
- You can have a **round**, **long** or **thin** face. You can have a **young** face or an **old** face.
- You can have a **big** head or a **small** head.
- Ears can also be **big** or **small**.
- We can also use adjectives of character for a face: he has a **kind** face; he has a **friendly** face; he has an **unfriendly** face.

Modifiers

+ +   Very

+   Quite

–   Not very

Be careful of word order.

She has a very beautiful face. ✔   **not:** She has very a beautiful face. ✗

He has quite a big nose. ✔   **not:** He has quite a nose big. ✗

He doesn't have a very big head. ✔   **not:** He doesn't have very a big head. ✗

We use body part + **too** + adjective to make the sentence sound negative.

☺ She has big eyes.

☹ His ears are **too** big.

Grammar notes

Singular and plural

Be careful to use the correct form.

Singular	**Plural**
He has **a** small nose.	He has large eyes. (**no** article)

Phrases

- He/she [has got/has] (a) + adjective + noun(s)
  Example: He has quite a young face, small ears, and lovely teeth.
- His/her + noun + is/are + adjective
  Example: Her nose is quite big.

Questions

- What [colour/color] is your hair/are your eyes?
- What is/are ... like?
  Example: What's her hair like? It's long, blond and curly.
  What are his eyes like? They're big and blue.

Practice

Exercise 1 The box below has nouns and adjectives. If you can use an adjective with a noun, put a ✔; if you cannot use that adjective with that noun, put a ✗.

	eyes	face	hair	lips
big	✔	✗	✗	✔
young				
thick				
blue				
small				
brown				
thin				
fair				

Exercise 2 Match the two parts of the sentences below.

1 She['s got/has] beautiful   a lips
2 She['s got/has] a big   b face
3 What [colour/color] are her eyes?   c beard
4 He [has got/has] quite a thin   d eyes
5 What's her hair like?   e brown
6 You['ve got/have] very thin   f nose
7 He [has got/has] a   g curly

Exercise 3 Look at the sentences below and decide if they are right or wrong. Then correct those that are wrong. For example:

You['ve got/have] a very thin face. ✔
He['s got/has] hair blond short. ✗   He['s got/has] short blond hair.

1 What [colour/color] is your eyes?
2 My father's hair is very [grey/gray].
3 I don't like my ears; they're too big.
4 I['ve got/have] a big quite head.
5 What is her face like?
6 She['s got/has] nice face, big blue eyes, and long dark hair.
7 Steve is a moustache and a beard.
8 I don't like beards; I'm clean-shaven.

Now check your answers.

▶ **Exercise 4 (Recordings 4.1, 4.2, 4.3, 4.4, 4.5)** Pronunciation practice. Listen and repeat the words on the recording. Use the transcript at the back of the book to help you if necessary.

In use

Reading

Before you start, check you know these words:

> famous   skin   intelligent   smile   unhappy

Note: A *portrait* is a picture of someone, especially their face; a *self-portrait* is a picture you make of yourself.

Portraits. Read the descriptions below from a magazine article describing two pictures. Don't worry about the words you don't know.

A

How do you describe one of the most famous faces in the world? There she sits, this mysterious woman. Everyone knows her face, but no-one knows who she was. So, where to start? Well, she has a round face with beautiful skin. It is quite a young face, but it is impossible to say how old she is. Her nose is quite big, but it is not too big. She also has big, brown eyes which look out of the picture and straight at you. The eyes look very intelligent, as though she knows what you're thinking. Her long, brown hair is quite thin and wavy. But it is her mouth that is most famous. Her thin lips are closed tightly together and she is smiling the most famous smile in the world.

B

He was one of the greatest artists the world has ever known, but he was so unhappy, and you can see that in his self-portraits. Now his face is famous. His head is not very big, but in this painting you can see a big left ear. He also has a big nose, while his blue eyes stare straight at you. You can see he's not a man at peace with the world. His mouth has thick lips and is closed. He has short, straight, red hair, as well as a beard and moustache. You can't help feeling sorry for this man.

Reading 1 Put the correct letter, A or B, next to each sentence below:

Which picture...
  has thick lips? *B*
  has brown eyes?
  has a beard and moustache?
  is unhappy?
  is a woman?
  has long hair?
  has a smile?
  has red hair?

Reading 2 Now take a piece of paper and try to draw the two faces. They are from two famous portraits – do you know who they are?

▶ Listening

Before you start, check you know these words:

funny	hate	make a joke	kind

Listen to this radio [programme/program] called *What's in a face?* Each week someone describes a picture and what it means to them.

Listening 1 (Recording 4.6) Listen to the recording and put the parts of the body below in the order in which you first hear them. Be careful – one part is *not* mentioned.

ear		face		mouth	
eye		hair	1	nose	

Listening 2 Put a ✔ next to the sentences you hear. Then listen to the recording again and see if you can correct the other sentences.

1 Well, his hair was still red then.
2 He has quite a thin face.
3 He's always hated his ears.
4 He has big blue eyes.
5 You see a really kind face.

Now check your answers.

Recap

Here are the words we learned in this unit. Do you know them all? Write down the translations if necessary.

Parts of the body

head	face	eye
nose	hair	ear
cheek	lip	mouth
tooth (teeth)		

Hair

long	short	straight
wavy	curly	bald
beard	moustache	clean-shaven

[Colours/Colors]

fair	dark	blond
brown	black	[grey/gray]
white	red	green
blue		

Qualities

| kind | friendly | unfriendly |

too + *adjective*

Size

| big | large | small |
| thick | thin | |

Shape and age

| round | young | old |

Questions

What [colour/color]...?   What is/are ... like?

What to do next

- Write a description of your own face.
- Write a description of a famous person's face – see if other people can guess who it is.
- Look at other faces and describe them in English.

Why not try these units next?

- Body (2) • Clothes (1) and (2) • People and jobs

Answer key for this unit

Test your basics

Check your answers on page 36 (Basics).

Exercise 1

	eyes	face	hair	lips
big	✔	✘	✘	✔
young	✘	✔	✘	✘
thick	✘	✘	✔	✔
blue	✔	✘	✘	✘
small	✔	✔	✘	✘
brown	✔	✘	✔	✘
thin	✘	✔	✔	✔
fair	✘	✘	✔	✘

Exercise 2

1 She['s got/has] beautiful eyes. (d)
2 She['s got/has] a big nose. (f)
3 What [colour/color] are her eyes? Brown. (e)
4 He [has got/has] quite a thin face. (b)
5 What's her hair like? Curly. (g)
6 You['ve got/have] very thin lips. (a)
7 He [has got/has] a beard. (c)

Exercise 3

1 What [colour/color] is your eyes? ✘
   What [colour/color] **are** your eyes?
2 My father's hair is very [grey/gray]. ✔
3 I don't like my ears; they're too big. ✔
4 I['ve got/have] a big quite head. ✘
   I['ve got/have] **quite a big** head.
5 What is her face like? ✔

6 She['s got/has] nice face, big blue eyes, and long dark hair. ✗
     She['s got/has] **a** nice face, big blue eyes, and long dark
     hair.
7 Steve is a moustache and a beard. ✗
     Steve **has** a moustache and a beard.
8 I don't like beards; I'm clean-shaven. ✔

Reading

Reading 1

Which picture:
    has thick lips? *B*
    has brown eyes? *A*
    has a beard and moustache? *B*
    is unhappy? *B*

is a woman? *A*
has long hair? *A*
has a smile? *A*
has red hair? *B*

Reading 2

Listening

Listening 1

ear	4	face	2	mouth	✗
eye	5	hair	1	nose	3

Listening 2

1 Well, his hair was still red then. ✗
     Well, his hair was still **brown** then.
2 He has quite a thin face. ✔
3 He's always hated his ears. ✗
     He's always hated his **nose**.
4 He has big blue eyes. ✔
5 You see a really kind face. ✔

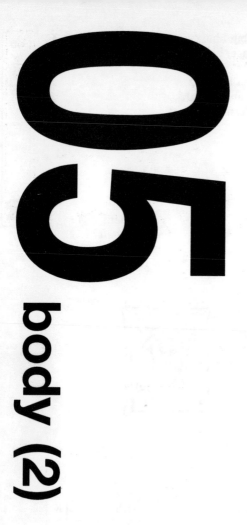

05

body (2)

In this unit you will learn
- parts of the body
- words for height, weight, appearance
- how to ask questions about/describe the body

Basics

Do you know these words? Check in a dictionary and write the word in your language.

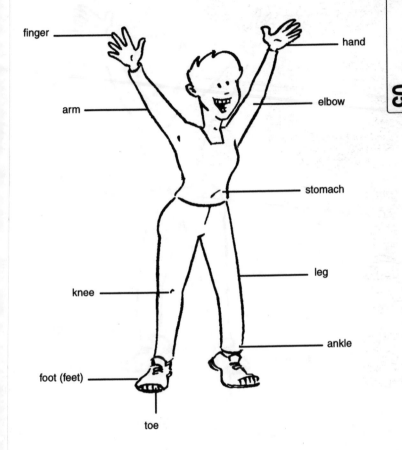

finger

hand

arm

elbow

stomach

leg

knee

ankle

foot (feet)

toe

Test your basics

Write the English word next to the picture below. Don't look at page 47!

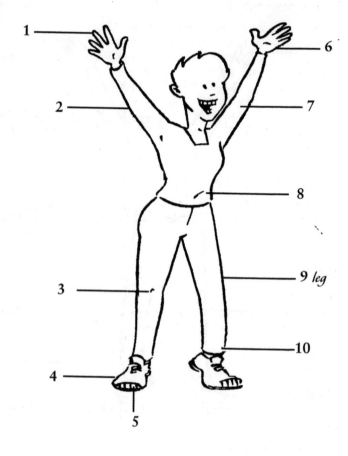

1

6

2

7

8

3

9 *leg*

4

10

5

Extension

General adjectives

Look at these opposites.

- People can be **tall** or they can be **short**.
- People can be **fair-skinned** or they can be **dark-skinned**.
- Race: people can be **black** (for example, African), **Asian** or **white**.
- People can be **good-looking**, or **beautiful** (for a woman) or **handsome** (for a man).
- People can be **overweight** (☺) or **fat** (☹); they can be **slim** (☺) or **thin** (☹). If people do a lot of sport, they may be **well-built**.

Arms, hands, fingers, legs, feet, toes

- Hands, feet and toes can be **big** or **small**.
- Arms, fingers and legs can be **long** or **short**; they can also be **fat** or **thin**.

Size

Weight (noun)

You **weigh** (verb) somebody when you want to know how **heavy** (adjective) he or she is. For example:

How heavy are you? or How much do you weigh?
I weigh 70kg.

Height (noun)

If you want to know someone's height, you ask how **tall** he or she is. For example:

How tall are you?
I'm 180cm tall.

Be careful! Britain and America use **pounds** for weight and **feet** and **inches** for height.

2.2 pounds = 1 kilogram
1 foot = 12 inches = 30 [centimetres/centimeters]

Questions

Do you remember the questions from Body (1)? If not, look again:

What [colour/color] is your hair? It's brown.
What's your hair like? It's long, straight, and brown.
What [colour/color] are your eyes? They're blue.
What are your eyes like? They're big and blue.

If we want a general description of someone, we can use the verb **look like**.

What do you look like? What does he/she look like?

This question needs a longer answer. Look at the box below for some ideas.

He's	very	thin	and	have got	blue	eyes	and	long	red	straight	hair.
She's	not very	tall		has got	brown			short	brown	curly	
I'm	quite	slim		[UK] or					[grey/gray]		
...		...		have	...			...	...	wavy	
				has [US]							

Practice

Exercise 1 Look at the square below and find seven words from this unit.

M	F	R	M	E	H	C	D	S
H	A	N	D	S	O	M	E	U
S	I	W	Z	F	D	P	Z	L
U	R	K	Y	A	V	L	O	O
E	S	H	O	R	T	R	S	N
J	K	O	P	L	E	I	B	G
S	I	F	T	P	F	N	Z	D
E	N	N	S	M	A	L	L	L
K	N	E	J	T	T	F	J	O
W	E	L	L	B	U	I	L	T
P	D	X	B	W	Y	O	Q	W

Exercise 2 Making questions. Put the words below into the correct order to make a question. For example:

what Tim look does like?   *What does Tim look like?*

1 how is heavy Jenny?
2 [colour/color] what Tim's is hair?
3 Jenny does what like look?
4 tall is how Tim?
5 is Jenny's hair what like?
6 [colour/color] Jenny's are eyes what?
7 weigh does Tim what?

Exercise 3 Look at the facts about Tim and Jenny. Then answer the questions in **Exercise 2** using this information.

Tim	Jenny
6 feet tall (180cm) 220 pounds (100kg) Short, dark, straight hair Big, green eyes	5 feet tall (150cm) 88 pounds (40kg) Quite good-looking Long, blond, curly hair Blue eyes

Example: What does Tim look like? He's tall, well-built, and [has got/has] short, dark, straight hair, and big, green eyes.

1 _____   5 _____

2 _____   6 _____

3 _____   7 _____

4 _____

Now check your answers.

▶ **Exercise 4 (Recordings 5.1, 5.2, 5.3, 5.4)** Pronunciation practice. Listen and repeat the words on the recording. Use the transcript at the back of the book to help you if necessary.

In use

Reading

Before you start, check you know these words:

| muscle farmer friends enemies ugly heart piano |

Below is the start of a story with a description of two people.

Reading 1 Look at the list below. In it you will see adjectives and nouns. Guess which adjectives go with which nouns. Then read the text and check your answers. There may be some words you don't know; don't worry about these.

thin   nose
big   fingers
small   hands
large   lips
long   eyes
brown   mouth

Glen Horrit stood up straight and, for the hundredth time that day, cursed the heat of the sun. Glen was quite a short man, and very well-built. But he wasn't fat. It was all muscle. He was a farmer and, like most farmers, was up early in the morning and not back in his bed until late at night. Glen had short, wavy hair which was already [grey/gray]. In another month, he would be forty, though he tried not to think about that. His eyes were still blue, though.

Glen smiled, though it was hard to see because he had such thin lips. All his features were small, except his big nose, and he certainly wasn't good-looking. His friends said he was plain; his enemies said he was ugly. His enemies were telling the truth. He had short legs and small hands, but his heart was big. And that was how he had got Ruth.

Ruth. His wife. His opposite. Ruth was tall and slim, and was still beautiful. Her long, straight hair was still red too – with a little bit of help from a bottle. Glen was an old-fashioned man, and to him Ruth was the perfect woman. She had a large mouth and round eyes that twinkled when she laughed. She was graceful too – Glen loved watching her long fingers as she played the piano. She was, even at thirty-eight, perfect to Glen. He didn't yet know the secret behind those soft brown eyes and beautiful face, and what his wife was really thinking of doing...

Reading 2 Read the true or false sentences below. Correct any that are false.

> **Examples:** Glen Horrit is tall. ✗ Glen Horrit is quite short.
> Ruth Horrit is tall. ✔

1 Glen has short, [grey/gray], curly hair.
2 Glen has thin lips.
3 Ruth has long fingers.
4 Some people think Glen is ugly.
5 Glen has blue eyes, but Ruth has green eyes.
6 Ruth has long, straight, red hair.
7 Glen is fat.
8 Ruth has a beautiful face with a small mouth and round eyes.

▶ Listening

Before you start, check you know these words:

> robbery   robber   jeans   sweater   T-shirt   trousers   shirt   gun

In the UK there is a television [programme/program] where people can give information to the police called 'Police – Help!'. Listen to part of the [programme/program] describing some robbers.

Listening 1 (Recording 5.4) One of the three men below is one of the robbers. Listen and then circle which one it is.

Tony	Steve	Jim
height: 5 feet 10	height: 5 feet 10	height: 5 feet 6
weight: about 200 pounds	weight: about 180 pounds	weight: 200 pounds
eyes: blue	eyes: brown	eyes: brown

Listening 2 Listen to the recording again and fill in the chart below.

	1st robber	2nd robber	3rd robber
height	_____	5 feet 6	_____
weight	200 pounds	_____	_____
hair	_____, dark	short, _____	_____
eye [colour/ color]	_____	_____	blue

Can you remember any other details about the robbers? Use the transcript to help you if necessary.

Now check your answers.

Recap

Here are the words we learned in this unit. Do you know them all? Write down the translations if necessary.

Parts of the body

leg	arm	hand
stomach	knee	finger
elbow	ankle	foot (feet)
toe		

Adjectives

tall	short	fair-skinned
dark-skinned	black	white
Asian	good-looking	beautiful
handsome	overweight	slim
well-built	thin	fat
big	small	long
short		

Size

weight	height	pound
kilogram	foot (feet)	inch
[centimetre/centimeter]		

Questions and answers

How heavy are you?	How much do you weigh?
I weigh …	How tall are you?
I'm …	What do you look like?

What to do next

- Describe yourself. Try recording your description on tape, and then write it down.
- Describe the people you see in pictures/paintings.
- Describe a member of your family.
- Describe someone famous and see if other people can guess who you mean.

Why not try these units next?

- Clothes (1) and (2) • Family • People and jobs

Answer key for this unit

Test your basics

Check your answers on page 47 (Basics).

Exercise 1

M	F	R	M	E	H	C	D	S
H	A	N	D	S	O	M	E	U
S	I	W	Z	F	D	P	Z	L
U	R	K	Y	A	V	L	O	O
E	S	H	O	R	T	R	S	N
J	K	O	P	L	E	I	B	G
S	I	F	T	P	F	N	Z	D
E	N	N	S	M	A	L	L	L
K	N	E	J	T	T	F	J	O
W	E	L	L	B	U	I	L	T
P	D	X	B	W	Y	O	Q	W

Exercise 2

1 How heavy is Jenny?
2 What [colour/color] is Tim's hair?
3 What does Jenny look like?
4 How tall is Tim?
5 What is Jenny's hair like?
6 What [colour/color] are Jenny's eyes?
7 What does Tim weigh?

Exercise 3

Possible answers:

1 She weighs 88 pounds.
2 It's dark.
3 She's quite short, quite good-looking, and she['s got/has] long, blond, curly hair and blue eyes.
4 He's 6 feet tall.
5 It's long, blond, and curly.
6 They're blue.
7 He weighs 220 pounds.

Reading

Reading 1

thin lips
big nose
small hands
large mouth
long fingers
brown eyes

Reading 2

1 Glen has short, [grey/gray], curly hair. ✗
    Glen has short, grey, **wavy** hair.
2 Ruth has thin lips. ✔
3 Ruth has long fingers. ✔
4 Some people think Glen is ugly. ✔

5 Glen has blue eyes, but Ruth has green eyes. ✗
  Glen has blue eyes, but Ruth has **brown** eyes.
6 Ruth has long, straight, red hair. ✔
7 Glen is fat. ✗   Glen is **well-built** (he isn't fat).
8 Ruth has a beautiful face with a small mouth and round eyes. ✗
  Ruth has a beautiful face, with a **large** mouth and round eyes.

Listening

Listening 1

(Tony)	Steve	Jim

height: 5 feet 10
weight: about
** 200 pounds**
eyes: blue
	height: 5 feet 10
	weight: about
	  180 pounds
	eyes: brown
		height: 5 feet 6
		weight:
		  200 pounds
		eyes: brown

Listening 2

	1st robber	2nd robber	3rd robber
height	6 *feet*	5 feet 6	*5 feet 10*
weight	200 pounds	*250 pounds*	*200 pounds*
hair	*long*, dark	short, [grey/gray]	*short, red*
eye [colour/ color]	*blue*	*brown*	blue

06

clothes (1)

In this unit you will learn
- the names of different clothes
- what verbs we use with clothes (put on, get dressed...)
- what clothes are singular/plural

Basics

Do you know these words? Check in a dictionary and write the word in your language.

1 sweater
(also: jumper, pullover)

7 T-shirt

2 shoes

8 shirt

3 boots

9 jacket

4 [trousers/pants]

10 coat

5 jeans

11 skirt

6 shorts

12 dress

Test your basics

Write the English word in the space provided. Don't look at page 59!

1

boots

_____

2

_____

3

_____

4

_____

5

_____

6

_____

7

_____

8

_____

9

_____

10

_____

11

_____

12

_____

Extension

More clothes

- A **hat** is something you wear on your head.
- A shirt for a woman can be called a **blouse**.
- Many men wear a **tie** with their shirt when they go to work.
- If you wear a matching jacket and [trousers/pants], we say you are wearing a **suit**. Most businessmen wear suits to work; a suit for a woman is often a jacket and a skirt, but she can wear a [**trouser suit/pantsuit**].
- [**Trainers/sneakers**] are shoes you wear for sport.
- On their feet, people often wear **socks** under their shoes.
- Under your [trousers/pants] you wear [**underpants/shorts**] (men) or [**knickers/panties**] (women); you can also wear a [**vest/undershirt**] under your shirt to keep you warm.
- Women also wear a **bra** (**brassière**) and often wear [**tights/pantyhose**] on their legs.
- In bed we wear **pyjamas**, some women wear a **nightdress** (**nightgown**).
- You can wear a **belt** for your [trousers/pants] and many women carry a [**handbag/purse**].
- We wear **earrings** on our ears, a **necklace** around our neck, a **bracelet** on our arms and **rings** on our fingers.

Make-up

- We can also wear **make-up**; many women wear make-up on their face.
- You put **lipstick** on your lips, **mascara** on your eyelashes, and **eye shadow** on your eyelids.
- We also use the verbs **put on**, **take off** and **wear** for make-up. For example:
  'Where's Jane?' 'She's putting on her lipstick.'
  I always wear make-up when I go out.
  The last thing I do at night is take off my make-up.

Verbs

- We use the verb **wear** to talk about clothes we have on. Be careful with your grammar. We use **wear** (Present Simple) to talk about what we do every day or routine; we use **am/are/is wearing** (Present Continuous) to talk about now. For example:

Normally I wear a dress to work, but today I'm wearing a [trouser suit/pantsuit].

- In the morning you **get dressed**, that is you **put on** your clothes. **Get dressed** means all your clothes, but we often use **put on** for one piece of clothing. For example:

    At eight o'clock I get dressed. First I put on my shirt, then I put my [trousers/pants] on.

- At night we use the opposite verbs, that is, you **get undressed** or **take off your clothes**. For example:

    I get undressed just before I go to bed. I take off my shirt and [trousers/pants] and put them away carefully.

- If you **change**, then you go from one set of clothes to another. For example:

    After work, I change from a shirt and tie to jeans and a T-shirt.

Note: Put on/take off/get dressed/get undressed/change. We use the Present Simple to describe what we do every day; we use the Present Continuous to describe the action if it's happening now and not finished. For example:

    I'll be there in a minute, I'm just getting dressed!
        (action now, unfinished)
    At bedtime, I change into my pyjamas. (routine)

Singular and plural

Clothes can be singular or plural: clothes that are plural normally have two parts. Look at the box below.

Singular	Plural
sweater, T-shirt, shirt, jacket, tie, skirt, dress, hat, blouse, suit, [trouser suit/pantsuit], vest, bra, pantyhose [US], nightdress, belt, [handbag/purse], necklace, bracelet, ring	shoes, boots, [trousers/pants], jeans, shorts, trainers, socks, [knickers/panties], tights [UK], [underpants/shorts], pyjamas, earrings

- With singular clothes we normally use **a/an**. For example: a shirt, a tie, a dress.
- We can also count singular clothes, for example: two shirts, three ties, four dresses.
- For plural clothes we use **pair of**. For example: a pair of [trousers/pants], a pair of shoes.
- We can also count plural clothes, for example: two pairs of [trousers/pants], three pairs of shoes.

Note: With the verb **wear**, we don't usually use the phrase **pair of**. For example: He's wearing a shirt and [trousers/pants].

Questions

- Asking for opinion
  What do you think of...?   I really like it/them.
  Do you like my...?   It's/They're really nice.
  Sorry, I don't like it/them much.

- Be careful of singular and plurals:

  Example:
  What do you think of my coat? I really like it.
  Do you like my shoes?   No, sorry I don't like them much.

Practice

Exercise 1 Complete the crossword with the correct words.

Clues

Down

1 It's cold! Put a ____ on over your shirt!
3 I know she's married, she has a ____ on her finger.
4 After work I always ____ into a T-shirt and jeans.
5 ____ dressed! It's time for school.
7 A shirt for a woman.
10 I need a new ____ of shoes.

Across

2 You wear a ____ on your arm.
6 Many women carry their make-up in their ____ (U.K.)
7 You often wear a ____ with [trousers/pants].
8 You wear a ____ around your neck.
9 I always wear a ____ to work.
11 She put her ____ on both ears.

Exercise 2 Choose the correct verb for each sentence. For example:

I get dressed/~~I'm getting dressed~~ at 7 o'clock every day.

1 Every night *I get undressed/I'm getting undressed* and then I have a shower.
2 I'm lucky, *I wear/I'm wearing* jeans to work.
3 'Where's Jackie?' '*She changes/She's changing* upstairs.'
4 If I have an important meeting, *I always wear/I'm always wearing* a suit.

5 You can't talk to Steve at the moment, *he gets dressed/he's getting dressed*.
6 *I put on/I'm putting on* a different tie every day.
7 Today, Marie *wears/is wearing* a [trouser suit/pantsuit] by Chanel.
8 'Hurry up!' 'All right, all right, *I just put on/I'm just putting on* my shoes.'

Exercise 3 Do you think the sentences below are correct? Correct any that you think have mistakes. For example:

John wears a skirt to work. ✗ John wears a suit to work.
I normally wear pyjamas to bed. ✔

1 'What do you wear at the weekend?' 'I normally wear a pair of jeans.'
2 'It's hot! Can I put my sweater on?' 'Of course.'
3 'What's Mike wearing today?' 'His new suit. Horrible, isn't it!'
4 'Do you like my [trousers/pants]?' 'Yes, I really like them.'
5 'What did you buy yesterday?' 'A pair of shoes. Do you like them?'
6 'Are you all right?' 'No, I think I need belt for these [trousers/pants].'
7 'Where's Sue?' 'She's putting on her lipstick. She won't be a minute.'
8 'What's the first thing you do when you come home from work?' 'Easy. I put on my clothes.'
9 'What's the American word for tights?' 'Socks.'
10 'What do you think of my dress?' 'Sorry, I don't really like them much.'

Now check your answers.

▶ **Exercise 4 (Recordings 6.1, 6.2, 6.3, 6.4, 6.5)** Pronunciation practice. Listen and repeat the words on the recording. Use the transcript at the back of the book to help you if necessary.

In use

Reading

Before you start, check you know these words:

| headache | wish | mirror | boring |

Here is a passage taken from a story. However, the sentences are all mixed up.

Reading 1 Put the sentences into the correct order.

	John took his pyjamas off, folded them, and put them on his bed ready for the night.
	Finally he put on a black pair of shoes and took his jacket off the door.
1	John woke with a bad headache and feeling sick. For a minute he almost stayed in bed, but he knew it was time to get dressed for work, so he got up slowly instead.
	He wished he could just change back into his pyjamas and go back to bed, but today was the first day of his new job, he couldn't miss it. With a sigh he walked out, closing his bedroom door behind him.
	He didn't have many clothes, so it didn't take him long to choose a tie and a dark pair of [trousers/pants].
	Next he walked over to his [wardrobe/closet]. He put on a white shirt then wondered what to put on next.
	John looked in the mirror at the clothes he was wearing and hated them; they looked so boring.

Reading 2 Are these sentences true (✔) or false (✗).

At the start of the story John was wearing pyjamas. ✔
John liked his work clothes. ✗ John didn't like his work clothes (he hated them).

1 John took his pyjamas off.
2 He put on a pair of [trainers/sneakers].
3 John had to get dressed to go out to a restaurant.
4 John wanted to change back into his pyjamas and go back to bed.
5 John put on a shirt, a pair of [trousers/pants], and a pair of shoes.
6 John put on a shirt before he put on his [trousers/pants].

▶ Listening

Note: A *credit card bill* tells us the amount of money we must pay back to a credit card company (like Visa or Mastercard).

You will hear a woman telling her husband about what she has bought.

Listening 1 (Recording 6.6) Listen and put a ✔ in the box below if she has bought these clothes.

blouse		boots		dress	
jacket		shoes		skirt	
sweater		[trousers/pants]		coat	

Listening 2 Listen to the recording again and write down how many she has bought of each item of clothing. If she hasn't bought any, put a cross (✗).

	blouse(s)		pair(s) of shoes
	pair(s) of boots		skirt(s)
	dress(es)		sweater(s)
	jacket(s)		pair(s) of [trousers/pants]

Now check your answers.

Recap

Here are the words we learned in this unit. Do you know them all? Write down the translations if necessary.

Clothes for the legs and feet

shoes	boots	[trousers/pants]
jeans	shorts	skirt
[trainers/sneakers]	socks	[underpants/shorts]
[knickers/panties]	[tights/pantyhose]	

Clothing for the rest of the body

sweater	T-shirt	shirt
jacket	coat	dress
hat	blouse	tie
suit	[trouser suit/pantsuit]	[vest/undershirt]
bra	pyjamas	nightdress (nightgown)

Extras

belt	[handbag/purse]	earrings
necklace	bracelet	ring

Make-up

lipstick	mascara	eye shadow

Verbs

wear	get dressed	get undressed
put on	take off	change

Singular and plural

a/an (a skirt, a jacket)
pair of (a pair of jeans, a pair of boots)

Questions

What do you think of...?   Do you like...?

I really like them. Sorry, I don't like it much.

What to do next

- Look at the clothes you are wearing – can you remember the English words for them all?
- Look in some [clothes shops/clothing stores] and test yourself on the clothes.
- Read a story and see how many clothes are described.

Why not try these units next?

• Clothes (2)   • Body (1) and (2)

Answer key for this unit

Test your basics

1

boots

2

coat

3

t-shirt

4

skirt

5

shoes

6

trousers

7

dress

8

sweater

9

shirt

10

shorts

11

jacket

12

jeans

Exercise 1

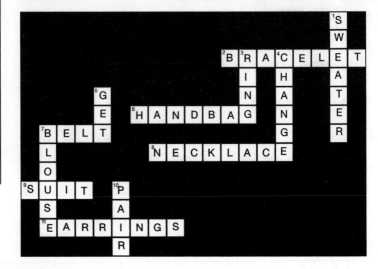

Exercise 2

1 Every night *I get undressed* and then I have a shower.
2 I'm lucky, *I wear* jeans to work.
3 'Where's Jackie?' '*She's changing* upstairs.'
4 If I have an important meeting, *I always wear* a suit.
5 You can't talk to Steve at the moment, *he's getting dressed*.
6 *I put on* a different tie every day.
7 Today, Marie *is wearing* a [trouser suit/pantsuit] by Chanel.
8 'Hurry up!' 'All right, all right, *I'm just putting* on my shoes.'

Exercise 3

1 'What do you wear at the weekend?' 'I normally wear a pair of jeans.' ✔
2 'It's hot! Can I put my sweater on?' 'Of course.' ✗
   'It's hot! Can I **take** my sweater **off**?' 'Of course.'
3 'What's Mike wearing today?' 'His new suit. Horrible, isn't it!' ✔
4 'Do you like my [trousers/pants]?' 'Yes, I really like them.' ✔
5 'What did you buy yesterday?' 'A pair of shoes. Do you like them?' ✔

6 'Are you all right?' 'No, I think I need belt for these [trousers/pants].' ✗

'Are you all right?' 'No, I think I need **a** belt for these [trousers/pants].

7 'Where's Sue?' 'She's putting on her lipstick. She won't be a minute.' ✔

8 'What's the first thing you do when you come home from work?' 'Easy. I put on my clothes.' ✗

'What's the first thing you do when you come home from work?' 'Easy. I **change** my clothes.'

9 'What's the American word for tights?' 'Socks.' ✗

'What's the American word for tights?' '**Pantyhose**'.

10 'What do you think of my dress?' 'Sorry, I don't really like them much.' ✗

'What do you think of my dress?' 'Sorry, I don't really like **it** much.'

Reading

Reading 1

2	John took his pyjamas off, folded them, and put them on his bed ready for the night.
5	Finally he put on a black pair of shoes and took his jacket off the door.
1	John woke with a bad headache and feeling sick. For a minute he almost stayed in bed, but he knew it was time to get dressed for work, so he got up slowly instead.
7	He wished he could just change back into his pyjamas and go back to bed, but today was the first day of his new job, he couldn't miss it. With a sigh he walked out, closing his bedroom door behind him.
4	He didn't have many clothes, so it didn't take him long to choose a tie and a dark pair of [trousers/pants].
3	Next he walked over to his [wardrobe/closet]. He put on a white shirt then wondered what to put on next.
6	John looked in the mirror at the clothes he was wearing and hated them; they looked so boring.

Reading 2

1 John took his pyjamas off. ✔
2 He put on a pair of [trainers/sneakers]. ✗ He put on a pair of **shoes**.
3 John had to get dressed to go out to a restaurant. ✗ John had to get dressed to go out to **work**.
4 John wanted to change back into his pyjamas and go back to bed. ✔
5 John put on a shirt, a pair of trousers, and a pair of shoes. ✗ John put on a shirt, **a tie**, a pair of [trousers/pants], and a pair of shoes.
6 John put on a shirt before he put on his [trousers/pants]. ✔

Listening

Listening 1

blouse	✔	boots	✔	dress	
jacket		shoes		skirt	✔
sweater	✔	[trousers/pants]	✔	coat	

Listening 2

3	blouse(s)	✗	pair(s) of shoes
1	pair(s) of boots	2	skirt(s)
✗	dress(es)	2	sweater(s)
✗	jacket(s)	1	pair(s) of [trousers/pants]

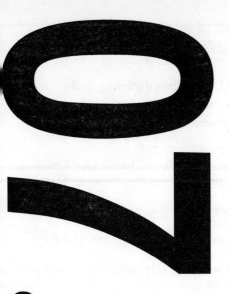

07

clothes (2)

In this unit you will learn
- how to choose and buy clothes (at the shops)
- words for pattern/material/style
- how to ask questions about/describe clothes

Basics

Note: It is a good idea to do Unit 6: Clothes (1) before you do this unit.

Do you know these words? Check in a dictionary and write the word in your language.

1 A [clothes shop/clothing store] sells clothes.
2 A [shoe shop/shoe store] sells shoes, boots, [trainers/ sneakers].
3 A **department store** sells all kinds of clothes and furniture; you can buy just about anything here (for example, Harrod's in London).
4 A **dry cleaner's** is a place where you get smart clothes (for example, a suit) cleaned.
5 A **changing room** is somewhere in the [shop/store] where you can try on clothes you want to buy.
6 **Lingerie** is clothes that women wear under their clothes – [knickers/panties], bra, etc.
7 **Accessories** are extras like belts, [handbags/purses], hats, etc.
8 [**Jewellery/jewelry**] includes earrings, necklaces, bracelets and rings.
9 **Cosmetics** means make-up (for example, lipstick, eye shadow, mascara).

Test your basics

Cover the words above so you can't see them. Then write the English word in the space provided.

1 You can try clothes on here.   *changing room*

2 This place sells shoes. _____

3 A place where you can buy [trousers/pants], skirts, dresses, etc. _____

4 This is a large shop where you can find just about anything. _____

5 This is where you can get smart clothes cleaned. _____

6 Earrings, necklace, bracelet, etc. are all... _____

7 Extras like belts or [handbags/purses] are... _____

8 Another word for make-up
(lipstick, eye shadow, etc.)   _____

9 [Knickers/panties], bra, etc.
are all...   _____

Extension

Describing clothes – adjectives

• Length: clothes (often for your legs) can be **long** or **short** (for
  example, skirts, dresses, and sometimes [trousers/pants].
• Size: clothes can also be **big** or **small** (for example, sweaters,
  shoes).
• Tightness: clothes can be **tight,** that is close to your skin or
  loose (for example, skirts, sweaters, trousers).

Pattern

• Clothes that have lines are **striped,** for example a blue and
  white striped shirt.
• Something that is **flowery** has flowers on it.
• Clothes can have [**spots/polka dots**] (noun), for example a
  blue tie with white [spots/polka dots].
• Don't forget that clothes can come in many [colours/colors] –
  for example **red, blue, green, black, white, brown;** we use the
  word **and** if something has more than one [colour/color], for
  example a black and white dress.

Material

• **Denim** is used to make jeans.
• **Wool** comes from sheep and is often used for sweaters.
• **Cotton** is a very useful material. It is often used for shirts and
  many other clothes.
• **Linen** is a slightly rough material made from flax.
• **Leather** comes from the skin of animals, and is often used for
  shoes, jackets or bags.
• **Silk** is a very soft, fine, expensive material.

General

• If clothes are **fashionable,** they are modern and up to date;
  the opposite is **unfashionable.**

- **Smart** clothes are in good condition. You often wear smart clothes for work, for example, a smart suit. **Scruffy** clothes are clothes that are dirty or in bad condition. **Casual** clothes are clothes you wear to relax, for example, jeans and a T-shirt. Casual is the opposite of smart.
- **Comfortable** clothes are easy to wear, for example, jeans; the opposite is **uncomfortable**.
- We can use the adjective **beautiful** to describe clothes, for example, a beautiful dress.
- Clothes you have had for a short time are **new**; **old** clothes are clothes you've had for a long time.

Word order

Look at the table to see what order we normally put adjectives in:

general	size	length	tightness	[colour/color]	pattern	material	clothes
fashionable beautiful new scruffy	big small	long short	tight loose	white blue blue and white	striped flowery	denim leather cotton	shirt dress shoes

Examples:

A horrible, blue, flowery shirt.
A fashionable, short, tight denim skirt.
A pair of striped trousers.

General adjectives and 'pair of...'

Be careful with the word order for **pair of**.
We normally put *new/old* before *pair of*: a new pair of brown leather shoes.
If we use a general adjective alone, we put it before; if we use more than one adjective, we often put it after. For example:

A nice pair of shoes.
A pair of nice, black leather shoes.

Questions and phrases

• Asking for a description

Note: If something *suits* you, you look good in it.

Questions	Response
How do I look?	You look great!
What do you think of...?	It really suits you./ They really suit you. It doesn't suit you./ They don't suit you.
What's/are your... like?	It's/They're long... made of...

• In a [shop/store]

Questions	Response
[Have you got/Do you have] a/any...?	Certainly. Come over here.
I'm looking for a/some...	Sorry, I'm afraid we [haven't got/don't have] any ...
I'd like a/some...	
Can I try it/them on?	Yes, of course./Sorry, I'm afraid you can't.
How much is/are...?	It's/They're...

Examples:

What's your new dress like?	It's long, blue and made from wool.
What do you think of these shoes?	They don't suit you.
Have you got any black jeans?	Certainly.
I'm looking for a blue silk shirt.	Sorry, I'm afraid we [haven't got/don't have] any.
Can I try on this skirt?	Yes, of course.
How much are these shoes?	Fifty dollars.

Practice

Exercise 1 See if you can find twelve words in the word square.

X	C	W	O	O	L	R	C	L	T	L	N
F	J	Q	V	X	C	F	L	O	B	M	E
A	E	L	O	O	S	E	D	N	E	S	W
S	B	E	K	U	M	P	W	G	M	I	P
H	F	A	P	S	U	I	T	Z	U	L	B
I	O	T	B	M	G	O	A	S	C	K	D
O	W	H	D	A	A	T	O	C	V	A	U
N	B	E	G	L	T	V	G	R	P	C	I
A	D	R	A	L	C	A	S	U	A	L	S
B	I	R	W	C	M	S	P	F	E	Y	C
L	L	B	E	A	U	T	I	F	U	L	T
E	A	U	N	L	L	I	M	Y	R	T	Q

(**Clue:** There are three types of material, eight adjectives and one verb that is also a type of clothing)

Exercise 2 Fill the gaps in each sentence with the words from the box below. Be careful, one of the words isn't used.

1 These [trousers/pants] are too ___*short*___; look, you can see my socks!
2 Where I live it's very hot, so I wear a lot of clothes made from _____ .
3 'You look very _____.' 'I have an important meeting at work today.'
4 That's a really _____ skirt. It suits you.
5 These shoes are quite _____, but they're really comfortable.
6 My [favourite/favorite] dress is black with red _____.
7 These [trousers/pants] are so _____, I can't walk.
8 His clothes are so _____, I think he still thinks it's the 1950s.
9 When I was younger, I had this great _____ jacket.

~~short~~	tight	big	[spots/polka dots]	denim
cotton	unfashionable	smart	nice	old

Exercise 3 Match a sentence or question in A with its reply in B.

A	B
1 How do I look in these jeans?	a It's blue and white striped and made of cotton.
2 What do you think of my new coat?	b Oh, they really suit you.
3 What's your new dress like?	c Certainly. The changing room is just over here.
4 I'm looking for some smart trousers.	d Certainly. I have a nice pair here.
5 I'd like a new suit.	e £60. Would you like to try it on?
6 Can I try these trousers on?	f I really like it. How much was it?
7 How much is this jacket?	g Of course. And do you need a tie to go with it?

Now check your answers.

▶ **Exercise 4 (Recordings 7.1, 7.2, 7.3, 7.4, 7.5)** Pronunciation practice. Listen and repeat the words on the recording. Use the transcript at the back of the book to help you if necessary.

In use

Reading

Note: If something is *in*, it's fashionable; if it's *out* it's unfashionable.

Below is a passage from a fashion magazine.

Reading 1 Look at the picture on the next page and put a ✔ next to the clothes the magazine believes are fashionable this year.

Ins and Outs – *Fashion with Sally Neemac*

What's in...

This season the look is for long, loose skirts, great to wear in the summer heat. Go for cotton or denim. The key to the look is to be comfortable.

What's out...

Don't wear short, tight skirts. That's so last year!

The dress has come back this year, I'm happy to say. Again, wear it long and comfortable in any material (silk is especially good).	Leather was the material of last year, so unless you ride motorbikes, forget it this year!
This season [trousers/pants] are like skirts – wear them long and loose and be comfortable. Striped [trousers/pants] are definitely in.	Shorts – do not wear these, even for sport! Flowery [trousers/pants] are definitely out.
[Trainers/sneakers] are the shoes to wear this season. And go for [colours/colors] – blue, green, brown – not boring white.	Don't wear your [trainers/sneakers] with socks. It's bare feet this season. And don't wear white, it's so unfashionable this year.
Men – dress smartly! Put on a suit and tie, and show the world you're successful.	Put away those scruffy jeans and T-shirts. This season's man is a winner, not a disaster!

Reading 2 Answer the questions about the passage in **Reading 1.**

1 What [colour/color] should you not wear this season?

   You shouldn't wear white.

2 What are [trousers/pants] like this season?
3 What clothes should men wear?
4 What materials are fashionable?
5 Which kinds of skirts are fashionable this season?

6 Should I wear striped [trousers/pants] or flowery [trousers/pants]?
7 What material was fashionable last year?
8 What should I wear on my feet? What should I not wear on my feet?

▶ Listening

You will hear three short conversations with Sally: one in a [clothes shop/clothing store], one in a shoe [shop/store], and one at home.

Listening 1 (Recording 7.6) Decide where each conversation is happening, and put the number of the conversation (1, 2, or 3) next to the clothes talked about. One item of clothing appears in two conversations; one item of clothing *isn't* used.

Where?	What clothes?	
at home ☐	boots ☐	suit ☐
[clothes shop/ clothing store] ☐	dress ☐3☐	sweater ☐
shoe [shop/store] ☐	jacket ☐	trainers ☐
	jeans ☐	

Listening 2 Listen to the recording again and put the words in the box next to the correct clothes. Be careful. Some clothes have more than one word and one item of clothing is *not* used.

boots _____
dress *wool, tight* _____
jacket _____
jeans _____
suit _____
sweater _____
trainers _____

£15	£60	£250	linen
leather	denim	~~wool~~	beautiful
~~tight~~	brown	green	black

Now check your answers.

Recap

Here are the words we learned in this unit. Do you know them all? Write down the translations if you need to.

Shops and departments

[clothes shop/clothing store]   [shoe shop/shoe store]
department store   changing room   dry cleaner's

Types of clothes and extras

lingerie   accessories   [jewellery/jewelry]
cosmetics

Length, size and tightness

| long | short | big |
| small | tight | loose |

Material

| denim | wool | cotton |
| linen | leather | silk |

Pattern

| striped | flowery | [spots/polka dots] |

General

fashionable	unfashionable	smart
scruffy	casual	comfortable
uncomfortable	great	beautiful
new	old	

Questions, phrases, and verbs

suit (someone)   How do I look?
What do you think of...?   What is/are your... like?
I'm looking for a/some...   I'd like a/some...
Can I try it/them on?   How much is/are?

What to do next

- Try to describe the clothes in your wardrobe – record yourself doing so.
- Look at magazine pictures and try to describe what people are wearing.
- Read a story in English and look carefully at descriptions of clothes; try to imagine those clothes in your head.
- Ask someone to describe their [favourite/favorite] clothes.
- Try describing clothes to a friend who must draw what you say – see how good the drawing is.

Why not try these units next?

- Body (1) and (2)   • People and jobs   • Shopping

Answer key for this unit

Test your basics

1	You can try clothes on here.	changing room
2	This place sells shoes.	shoe [shop/store]
3	A place where you can buy [trousers/pants], skirts, dresses, etc.	[clothes shop/ clothing store]
4	This is a large shop where you can find just about anything.	department store
5	This is where you can get smart clothes cleaned.	dry cleaner's
6	Earrings, necklace, bracelet, etc. are all…	[jewellery/jewelry]
7	Extras like belts or [handbags/purses] are…	accessories
8	Another word for make-up (lipstick, eye shadow, etc.)	cosmetics
9	[Knickers/panties], bra, etc. are all…	lingerie

Exercise 1

X	C	W	O	O	L	R	C	L	T	L	N
F	J	Q	V	X	C	F	L	O	B	M	E
A	E	L	O	O	S	E	D	N	E	S	W
S	B	E	K	U	M	P	W	G	M	I	P
H	F	A	P	S	U	I	T	Z	U	L	B
I	O	T	B	M	G	O	A	S	C	K	D
O	W	H	D	A	A	T	O	C	V	A	U
N	B	E	G	L	T	V	G	R	P	C	I
A	D	R	A	L	C	A	S	U	A	L	S
B	I	R	W	C	M	S	P	F	E	Y	C
L	L	B	E	A	U	T	I	F	U	L	T
E	A	U	N	L	L	I	M	Y	R	T	Q

Exercise 2

1 These [trousers/pants] are too *short*; look, you can see my socks!
2 Where I live it's very hot, so I wear a lot of clothes made from *cotton*.
3 'You look very *smart*.' 'I have an important meeting at work today.'
4 That's a really *nice* skirt. It suits you.
5 These shoes are quite *old*, but they're really comfortable.
6 My [favourite/favorite] dress is black with red [spots/polka dots].
7 These [trousers/pants] are so *tight*, I can't walk.
8 His clothes are so *unfashionable*, I think he still thinks it's the 1950s.
9 When I was younger, I had this great *denim* jacket.

(The adjective *big* is not used.)

Exercise 3

	A		B
1	How do I look in these jeans?	b	Oh, they really suit you.
2	What do you think of my new coat?	f	I really like it. How much was it?
3	What's your new dress like?	a	It's blue and white striped and made of cotton.
4	I'm looking for some smart [trousers/pants].	d	Certainly. I have a nice pair here.
5	I'd like a new suit.	g	Of course. And do you need a tie to go with it?
6	Can I try these [trousers/pants] on?	d	Certainly. The changing room is just over here.
7	How much is this jacket?	e	£60. Would you like to try it on?

Reading

Reading 1

Reading 2

1 You shouldn't wear white.
2 Long and loose (like skirts).
3 Men should wear smart clothes, suits and ties.
4 Cotton and denim (for skirts); silk for dresses.
5 Long, loose skirts.
6 Striped [trousers/pants].
7 Leather was fashionable last year.
8 You should wear [trainers/sneakers]; you should not wear socks.

Listening

Listening 1

Where?	What cloths?	
at home *3*	boots *2, 3*	suit *1*
[clothes shop/ *1* clothing store]	dress *3*	sweater *1*
shoe [shop/store] *2*	jacket ✗	trainers *3*
	jeans *3*	

Listening 2

boots	*beautiful, brown, leather, £250*
dress	*wool, tight*
jacket	✗
jeans	*black*
suit	*linen*
sweater	*green, £15*
trainers	*£60*

(*denim* is not used.)

08

drinks

In this unit you will learn
- the names of many drinks
- words to describe drinks
- how to ask for/offer a drink

Basics

Do you know these words? Check in a dictionary and write the word in your language.

1 water

2 milk

3 tea

4 coffee

5 (hot) chocolate

6 orange juice

7 beer

8 wine

9 [whisky/whiskey]

Test your basics

Cover the words on page 88 so you can't see them. Then write the English words.

1

hot chocolate

2

3

4

5

6

7

8

9

Extension

Types of drinks

Hot drinks

- You can drink your tea and coffee with milk or **cream**; we call this a **white** coffee or tea; without milk or cream we call it **black**.
- Some people drink tea with **lemon** and no milk.
- Some people like to have **sugar**.

Note: Some people also like to drink hot milk.

Cold drinks

- A drink can be [**fizzy/carbonated**] (like Coca-Cola) or **still** (like orange juice).
- Drinks without alcohol are called **soft** drinks.
- [Fizzy drinks/sodas]: **tonic, Coca-Cola**.

Note: In Britain **lemonade** is a [fizzy/carbonated] drink but in the US it is still (not [fizzy/carbonated]).

- Fruit juices: **pineapple juice, grapefruit juice, apple juice**.
- People often put **ice** in cold drinks to make them cooler.

Note: Some people also like to drink **iced** coffee or tea.

Alcoholic drinks

- We can have **red, white** or **rosé** wine.
- Beer: in Britain people drink **bitter** or **lager**; bitter is a darker beer than lager. It's all called beer in America.
- Spirits are drinks such as [**whisky/whiskey**], **brandy, vodka, gin**.

Amounts

- We have a **glass** of fruit juice or lemonade or wine but a **cup** of tea/coffee.
- You can also have a **pot** of tea or coffee (a pot has a few cups of tea or coffee in it).
- In Britain you can buy a **pint** of beer or **half a pint**; in Europe you can buy a [**litre/liter**], or **half a** [**litre/liter**] of beer.
- You can also buy wine and beer in **bottles**.

Places to drink

- You can have a drink with a meal in a **restaurant**.
- A [café/coffee shop] is a place that sells lighter food as well as hot and cold drinks, but not normally alcoholic drinks.
- A [pub/bar] sells alcoholic drinks as well as soft drinks.
- A **bar** is another place to buy alcoholic drinks; this is often part of another building, for example part of a hotel. In the US it is the name for a pub.

Questions and sentences

- If you're **thirsty**, it means you want a drink; you can ask if someone is thirsty.

  I'm thirsty.
  Are you thirsty? Yes, I am./No, I'm not.

- If you ask for a drink, you can say **I'd like a/two/three...** + drink(s).
- You can also say **Could I have...?**

  I'd like a coffee, please.   *Could I have a coffee, please?*

  I'd like two lemonades and an orange juice, please.   *Could I have two lemonades and an orange juice, please?*

- You can ask what someone wants using: **What would you like?** *What would you like?* I'd like a coffee, please.
- You can say **What would you like?** in a [shop/store] or in a house. If you are offering someone a drink in your house, you can also say **What can I get you?** or **Would you like...?**

  What can I get you? A glass of water, please.

  Would you like a drink? Yes, please. An orange juice.

  Would you like some tea? No, thanks.

- You can give a choice using **Would you like/prefer... or...?**

  Would you prefer tea or coffee? Coffee, please.

  Would you like black coffee or coffee with cream? With cream, please.

Practice

Exercise 1 Put the words from the box below into the table. Some words can go under more than one heading.

[café/coffee shop]   water   tea   [litre/liter]   restaurant
cup   hot chocolate   lager   pineapple juice
glass   milk   [whisky/whiskey]   coffee   pub   tonic   pint

cold drinks	hot drinks	fizzy/ carbonated	alcoholic drinks	amounts	places
					[café/ coffee shop]

Exercise 2 Fill the gaps with a suitable word for each noun.

	1 *w*	*h*	*i*	*t*	7 *e*			
2								
				3				
				4				
			5					
		6						

1 _____ wine
2 _____ juice
3 _____ Coca-Cola (British)
4 _____ drinks
5 _____ chocolate
6 a _____ of beer (US)

Now take the six letters from the middle of the word sequence and make the name of a drink, for example:

ealmnoed   *lemonade*

7 _____

Exercise 3 Match the question/sentence to its correct response.

1	What would you like?	OK, what can I get you?
2	Are you thirsty?	Coffee, please.
3	I'm thirsty.	Certainly. Would you like it black or with cream?
4	I'd like a coffee, please.	I'd like an orange juice, please.
5	Would you like a glass of water?	Of course. Would you like ice with that?
6	Would you prefer tea or coffee?	Yes, I am. Have you got anything to drink?
7	Could I have a glass of lemonade, please?	Oh yes, please. I'm very thirsty.
8	What can I get you?	A glass of red wine, please.

Now check your answers.

▶ **Exercise 4 (Recordings 8.1, 8.2, 8.3, 8.4, 8.5)** Pronunciation practice. Listen and repeat the words on the recording. Use the transcript at the back of the book to help you if necessary.

In use

Reading

Before you start, check you know these words:

Asia   Indonesia (adj. Indonesian)   island   mango

Note: The 1600s are the years 1600–1699.

Sonny Jim's...

Drinks Menu

13 Java Mix

Drink in the rich, dark, aromatic taste of Asia! Made from the finest beans available on this exotic Indonesian island, our blend is guaranteed to keep you awake. You can have it with milk, but Sonny Jim recommends drinking it black, in a double, extra large mug, but not before bedtime. You'll never go to sleep!

31 Fruit Slush

Pineapple, grapefruit, orange, and mango are all mixed together to make this long, refreshing cool drink. Have it with ice, in our special Sonny Jim's tall glass, but, order early on a hot day, because this wicked mix sells *fast*.

33 Sonny Jim's Export

Sonny Jim's full strength lager, brewed locally. Sonny Jim has been brewing since 1973, producing a range of lagers and bitters that are without equal. And this is our king of lagers, the strongest drink we make! Drink it ice cold in our special Sonny Jim's pint glass!

47 Count Black's Cold T

Hot? Need a drink that will attack your thirst quickly? Count Black first made his Cold T for the drinkers of London back in the 1600s, and Sonny Jim's is proud to be bringing that recipe back for the drinkers of today. Made from a mix of Indian and Chinese leaves, Count Black's Cold T must be drunk *cold*. Sounds awful? Don't knock it till you try it (we think you'll love it!) Whatever you do, don't add milk!

Look at the menu on page 94 from Sonny Jim's, a new bar and café in Manchester.

Reading 1 Match the name of the drink to the type of drink it is (one type isn't used).

Drink	Type
Java Mix	beer
Fruit Slush	coffee
Sonny Jim's Export	fruit juice
Count Black's Cold T	milk
	tea

Reading 2 Now answer these questions about the drinks.

1 Where does Java Mix come from?

The island of Java (part of Indonesia, in Asia).

2 When should you *not* drink Java Mix? Why not?
3 Which fruits make up Fruit Slush?
4 When is this drink popular?
5 What kind of beer is Sonny Jim's Export?
6 What's the best way to have Sonny Jim's Export?
7 When did people first drink Count Black's Cold T?
8 How should you drink Count Black's Cold T, and how should you not drink it?
9 Which of the drinks are cold drinks?
10 Which of the drinks are hot drinks?
11 Which of the drinks are alcoholic drinks?
12 Which of the drinks are [fizzy/carbonated] drinks?

▶ Listening

You are going to hear four conversations with people asking for drinks.

Listening 1 (Recording 8.6) Listen to the recording and put the number of the conversation next to the location.

home	☐	pub	☐
restaurant	☐	[café/coffee shop]	☐

Listening 2 Look at the sentences below. Write the number of the conversation next to each line. There are two sentences from each conversation; one sentence is *not* used.

1 I'd like a pint of beer, please ☐

2 Would you like something to drink? 1

3 And what would you like to drink? ☐

4 Yes, I think we'd like a bottle of wine, please. ☐

5 ...could we have two glassses of water as well, please? ☐

6 ...what can I get you? ☐

7 White, please. With two sugars. ☐

8 I think it has to be red. ☐

9 Just a glass of lemonade, please. ☐

Now check your answers.

Recap

Here are the words we learned in this unit. Do you know them all? Write down the translations if you need to.

Cold drinks

water   milk   orange juice
lemonade   tonic   Coca-Cola
pineapple juice grapefruit juice   apple juice
ice

Hot drinks

tea (with lemon/milk/cream)   (hot) chocolate
coffee (with milk/cream)   sugar

Alcoholic drinks

beer   wine   spirits
bitter   lager   [whisky/whiskey]
brandy   vodka   gin

Adjectives

[fizzy/carbonated]	still	soft
black (coffee)	white (coffee)	red (wine)
white (wine)		

Amounts

glass	cup	pot
pint	half a pint	[litre/liter]
half a [litre/liter]	bottle	

Questions and sentences

I'm thirsty	Are you thirsty?	I'd like...
Could I have...?	Would you like a...?	Would you prefer... or...?
What would you like?	What can I get you?	

Places to drink

restaurant	[café/coffee shop]	pub
bar		

What to do next

- Try asking for your [favourite/favorite] drink.
- Describe a new drink for Sonny Jim's menu.

Why not try this unit next?

- Food (1) • Shopping

Answer key for this unit

Test your basics

1 (hot chocolate)

2 wine

3 milk

4 orange juice

5 beer

6 water

7 tea

8 [whisky/whiskey]

9 coffee

Exercise 1

cold drinks	hot drinks	fizzy/ carbonated	alcoholic drinks	amounts	places
water, tea, pineapple juice, coffee, tonic, milk	*tea, coffee, milk, hot chocolate*	*water, tonic*	*lager, [whisky/ whiskey]*	*[litre/ liter], cup, pint, glass*	*[café/ coffee shop], restaurant, pub*

Exercise 2

	1 w	h	i	t	7 e				
2 g	r	a	p	e	f	r	u	i	t
				3 f	i	z	z	y	
				4 c	o	l	d		
		5 h	o	t					
	6 l	i	t	e	r				

7 coffee

Exercise 3

1 What would you like? — I'd like an orange juice, please.

2 Are you thirsty? — Yes, I am. Have you got anything to drink?

3 I'm thirsty. — OK, what can I get you?

4 I'd like a coffee, please. — Certainly. Would you like it black or with cream?

5 Would you like a glass of water? — Oh yes, please. I'm very thirsty.

6 Would you prefer tea or coffee? — Coffee, please.

7 Could I have a glass of lemonade, please? — Of course. Would you like ice with that?

8 What can I get you? — A glass of red wine, please.

Reading

Reading 1

Drink	Type
Java Mix	coffee
Fruit Slush	fruit juice
Sonny Jim's Export	beer
Count Black's Cold T	tea

(*milk* is not used)

Reading 2

1 The island of Java (part of Indonesia, in Asia).
2 You shouldn't drink Java Mix at bedtime. You won't go to sleep.
3 Pineapple, grapefruit, orange, and mango.
4 On a hot day (it sells fast).
5 Sonny Jim's Export is a lager.
6 It's best to drink Sonny Jim's Export ice cold in a special Sonny Jim's pint glass.
7 People first drank Count Black's Cold T in the 1600s.
8 You should drink it cold. You should not drink it with milk.
9 Fruit Slush, Sonny Jim's Export, and Count Black's Cold T.
10 Java Mix.
11 Sonny Jim's Export.
12 None of them!

Listening

Listening 1

| home | 1 | pub | 4 |
| restaurant | 2 | [café/coffee shop] | 3 |

Listening 2

1 I'd like a pint of beer, please. [x]

2 Would you like something to drink? [1]

3 And what would you like to drink? [3]

4 Yes, I think we'd like a bottle of wine, please. [2]

5 ...could we have two glasses of water as well, please? [3]

6 ...what can I get you? [4]

7 White, please. With two sugars. [1]

8 I think it has to be red. [2]

9 Just a glass of lemonade, please. [4]

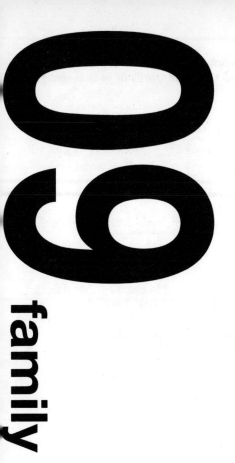

09

family

In this unit you will learn
- words for members of the family
- how to ask questions about a family
- how to talk about your own family

Basics

Look at the family tree below. Do you know the words in bold?
Check in a dictionary and write the words in your language.

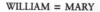

WILLIAM = MARY

My name's William.
I'm Paul and Lucy's
grandfather.

My name's Mary.
I'm Paul and Lucy's
grandmother.

JAMES = SARAH

My name's
James.
I'm Paul and
Lucy's **father**.

My name's
Sarah. I'm
Paul and
Lucy's **mother**.

MARK = HELEN

My name's
Mark. I'm
Helen's
husband.

My name's
Helen. I'm
Mark's **wife**.

PAUL

My name's
Paul. I'm
James and
Sarah's **son**
and
William and
Mary's
grandson.

LUCY

My name's
Lucy. I'm
James and
Sarah's **daughter**
and
William and
Mary's
granddaughter.

TINA

My name's
Tina. I'm
Simon's
sister.

SIMON

My name's
Simon. I'm
Tina's
brother.

Test your basics

Look again at the family tree, then write the English words in the spaces below.

WILLIAM = MARY

My name's William.
I'm Tina and Simon's
1 _____.

My name's Mary.
I'm Tina and Simon's
2 _____.

JAMES = SARAH   MARK = HELEN

My name's   My name's   My name's   My name's
James.   Sarah. I'm   Mark. I'm   Helen. I'm
I'm Sarah's   James's   Tina and   Tina and
                                      Simon's   Simon's

3 _____.   4 _____.   5 _____.   6 _____.

PAUL   LUCY   TINA   SIMON

My name's   My name's   My name's   My name's
Paul. I'm   Lucy. I'm   Tina. I'm   Simon. I'm
Lucy's   Paul's   Mark and   Mark and
                                Helen's   Helen's

7 _____.   8 _____.   9 _____ and 11 _____ and
                                William and   William and
                                Mary's   Mary's
                                10 _____.   12 _____.

Extension

More family

Look again at the family tree in Basics to help you understand these family words.

- Your father and your mother are your **parents**; we normally use the informal words **dad** for father and [**mum/mom**] for mother.
- Mark is Paul and Lucy's **uncle**; Helen is Paul and Lucy's **aunt**.
- Simon is James and Sarah's **nephew**; Tina is James and Sarah's **niece**.
- Paul and Lucy and Tina and Simon are **cousins** (same word for male and female).
- James is Mark's **brother-in-law**; Sarah is Helen's **sister-in-law**; William is James and Helen's **father-in-law** and Mary is their **mother-in-law**.
- If two children have one parent the same and one different, we use the prefix **half**, for example, *she's my half-sister; we both have the same mother but we have different fathers.*
- If a parent remarries, then you might have **step** relations.
  Example: My father has remarried so I now have a *stepmother.*
- Mother, father, sister, brother, brother-in-law, daughter, etc. – all these words are types of **relation**.

Marriage

- James and Sarah **are married**; we use **get married** for the day of the wedding, for example:
  James and Sarah *got married* ten years ago.
- We use the Present Perfect with the verb *be* to say how long you've been married, for example:
  William and Mary *have been married* for 48 years.
- If your husband or wife dies, then you are **widowed** (adj.). If you are a woman, you are a **widow**, if you are a man, you are a **widower**. For example:
  Are you married? No, I'm *widowed.*

  My uncle's a *widower.*

- If a marriage breaks up, there's often a **divorce** (adjective = **divorced**); you can use the prefix **ex** to talk about your previous husband or wife, for example:
  James has an *ex-wife* called Charlotte.
- If you are not married, then you are **single**.

Children

- We normally use **have children** to mean 'possession'. For example:

  We have three children (possession).

- We use **have a baby** to mean 'give birth'. For example:

  She's having a baby in June (give birth).

- When a child has no brothers or sisters, we can say he/she is an **only child**.

- We often talk about **older** or **younger** brothers or sisters, for example:

  Tina is Simon's older sister; Mark is Sarah's younger brother.

- We can use the word [**favourite/favorite**] about a relation you like the most, for example:

  Alice is Sarah's [favourite/favorite] niece.

Questions

- Use **Have you got any...?** to ask about someone's family.
- **How many ... have you got?** or **How many ... do you have?** asks about the number.
- **Is your ... older/younger than you?**
- **Are you married/single/widowed/divorced?** (Normally we use **Are you married?**) (Remember also **When did you get married?** and **How long have you been married?**)
- We can ask simply **Do you like your...?** to ask about family likes/dislikes. **Who's your [favourite/favorite] ...?** asks about who you like the most.

  Examples:

Have you got any children?	Yes, I have./No, I haven't.
How many children do you have?	I have two (children).
Is your brother older than you?	Yes, he is./No, he isn't.
Are you married?	Yes, I am./No, I'm not. I'm, single/divorced/widowed.
Do you like your younger sister?	Yes, I do./No, I don't.
Who's your [favourite/favorite] aunt?	Aunt Helen. She's great!

Practice

Exercise 1 In the word box there are six pairs of relation words, male and female. Find the pairs, then write them in the correct spaces in the box below.

R	F	S	B	I	M	O	W	I	D	O	W
C	A	W	M	U	L	V	I	H	C	N	C
E	U	O	X	W	I	A	F	V	O	E	U
T	N	D	B	G	U	Z	E	W	T	P	M
I	T	H	C	H	U	N	C	L	E	H	R
M	B	K	O	P	S	E	M	G	J	E	F
N	C	O	U	S	I	N	A	N	K	W	H
I	R	O	S	L	H	U	S	B	A	N	D
E	J	N	I	N	J	D	O	E	L	N	S
C	I	R	N	Y	Z	S	O	N	B	A	D
E	D	Q	T	A	C	G	O	N	V	E	X
A	D	A	U	G	H	T	E	R	S	U	D
W	I	D	O	W	E	R	D	U	V	E	Z

Male	Female
uncle	*aunt*

Exercise 2 Fill in the missing words in the questions or answers below using the words from the box. Be careful, one word is not used.

1 When did you get *married*? Three years ago. It was a lovely day!
2 My sister has two children. I have a _____ called Sarah, she's 12 years old, and a _____ called Daniel, who's 10.
3 My [mum/mom] married again three years ago, and last year she and my stepfather had a boy, he is my _____.
4 Poor Aunt Jane. She was _____ last year when her husband died, she still misses him.
5 'Do you like your _____?' 'I can't say. Both my wife's parents died before I met her.'

6 Even though we were _____ five years ago, I'm still good friends with my _____.

7 'Do you ever want to get married?' 'No thanks, I want to stay _____ – it's much more fun!'

107

family

09

divorced ex-wife half-brother ~~married~~ mother-in-law

niece nephew single stepbrother widowed

Exercise 3 Match the questions to the answers.

1 Have you got any cousins? a No, I'm not. I'm single.

2 Is your sister older than you? b No, she isn't. She's two years younger.

3 How many brothers and sisters have you got? c My Aunt Polly. She's great. She's so much fun.

4 Are you married? d Yes, I have. I have two cousins.

5 Do you like your brother? e I've got one brother and one sister.

6 Who's your [favourite/favorite] relation? f No, I don't really like him, although I do like my sister.

Now check your answers.

▶ **Exercise 4** (Recordings 9.1, 9.2, 9.3, 9.4, 9.5) Pronunciation practice. Listen and repeat the words on the recording. Use the transcript at the back of the book to help you if necessary.

In use

Reading

Before you start, check you know these words:

scruffy waste (time) laugh joke horror

Here is a short piece from a novel called *Marrying William*. In it Kate, who is going to marry William, meets William's mother (Mrs. Saunders) for the first time.

Reading 1 Read the text and write down what family Mrs. Saunders has.

"I," said a lady in her fifties, "am William's mother."

I shook her hand, feeling terribly scruffy in my jeans and T-shirt.

"Hi," I said. "My name's Kate."

"I know," said Mrs. Saunders. She didn't waste any time. "Tell me about yourself, Kate. Tell me about your family." Oh dear. This could take some time.

"Well, I come from quite a big family, actually. I have eight brothers and sisters. I'm the youngest. After me, they decided to stop, fast!" (Mrs. Saunders did not laugh at my joke, so I carried on.) "Anyway, most of my brothers and sisters are married now. I have, er, twelve nephews and nine nieces… I think. Yes, that's right, and my brother George and his wife are having their baby next month, so that will be another one. It's terrible for birthdays, especially for my poor grandmother." (That's my [mum's/mom's] mother, my [mum/mom] was her only child.) "She has to keep a list to help her remember."

I looked at the horror in Mrs. Saunders' face and stopped. She could see William disappearing into this huge family of mine. I decided not to tell her how my father had married again and about my new half-brother who lived in Spain. I didn't tell her either about my two stepsisters, from my stepfather's first marriage. And I certainly didn't tell her about my own ex-husband, who lives in London somewhere.

"What about your family, Mrs. Saunders?" I tried.

"William is an only child," she said, "like myself. And I have been a widow for sixteen years."

"Ah," I said, guiltily. What else could I say?

Reading 2 Look at the statements below and decide if they are true (✔) or false (✘), then correct those that are false.

1 Kate's grandmother is the mother of Kate's [mum/mom]. ✔
2 Kate is married. ✘ Kate is divorced (she has an ex-husband who's still alive). She's getting married to William in the future.

3 Kate's mother and father are married.
4 Kate's brother George's new child will have twenty-one cousins.
5 Mrs. Saunders is a widower.
6 Kate's brothers and sisters are all older than she is, but her half-brother is younger.
7 Kate's stepfather has two sisters.
8 William has no father.
9 Kate's brothers and sisters have had more sons than daughters.
10 Kate's grandmother has eight grandchildren.

▶ Listening

Before you start, check you know this word:

> insurance

Note: *Related by blood* means you are from the same family, you're not related by marriage. For example: Your mother is a blood relation; your mother-in-law or your stepmother are not blood relations.

You will hear a woman being interviewed by a man selling insurance.

Listening 1 Listen and put a ✓ next to any questions below that you hear.

1 Are you married? ☐

2 Have you got any children? ☐

3 Who's your [favourite/favorite] relation? ☐

4 Is your brother older or younger than you? ☐

5 What about your parents, are they still alive? ☐

Listening 2 Listen again and fill in the form with any details about the woman's family.

Name	*Marion Jacobs*
Marital status*	*Single*
Children	
Parents	
Brothers	
Sisters	

* married, divorced, widowed or single

Now check your answers.

Recap

Here are the words we learned in this unit. Do you know them all? Write down the translations if you need to.

Family

dad (informal)	father (formal)	[mum/mom] (informal)
mother (formal)	son	daughter
brother	sister	grandfather
grandmother	grandson	granddaughter
uncle	aunt	cousin
nephew	niece	wife
husband	parents	brother-in-law
sister-in-law	half-sister	stepmother
relation		

Marriage

be married	get married	married
widowed	widower	widow
divorced	single	ex-husband/wife

Children

have children (possession)
only child   older

have a baby (give birth)
younger

Questions

Have you got any ...?
How many ... have you got?

Do you have any...?
How many ... do you
    have?

Is your ... older/younger than you?
(Also: are you single/widowed/divorced?)
Do you like your ...?

Are you married?

Who's your [favourite/
    favorite] ...?

What to do next

- Describe your family in English.
- Ask someone about their family in English.
- Can you describe any famous families in books? Politics?
  Music?

Why not try these units next?

- Body (1) and (2)   • Clothes (1) and (2)   • People and jobs

Answer key for this unit

Test your basics

1 grandfather	2 grandmother
3 husband	4 wife
5 father	6 mother
7 brother	8 sister
9 daughter	10 granddaughter
11 son	12 grandson

Exercise 1

R	F	S	B	I	M	O	W	I	D	O	W
C	A	W	M	U	L	V	I	H	C	N	C
E	U	O	X	W	I	A	F	V	O	E	U
T	N	D	B	G	U	Z	E	W	T	P	M
I	T	H	C	H	U	N	C	L	E	H	R
M	B	K	O	P	S	E	M	G	J	E	F
N	C	O	U	S	I	N	A	N	K	W	H
I	R	O	S	L	H	U	S	B	A	N	D
E	J	N	I	N	J	D	O	E	L	N	S
C	I	R	N	Y	Z	S	O	N	B	A	D
E	D	Q	T	A	C	G	O	N	V	E	X
A	D	A	U	G	H	T	E	R	S	U	D
W	I	D	O	W	E	R	D	U	V	E	Z

Male	Female
uncle	aunt
nephew	niece
son	daughter
husband	wife
widower	widow
cousin	cousin

(**Note:** *cousin* is the same for male and female.)

Exercise 2

1 When did you get *married*? Three years ago. It was a lovely day!
2 My sister has two children. I have a *niece* called Sarah, she's 12 years old, and a *nephew* called Daniel, who's 10.

3 My [mum/mom] married again three years ago, and last year she and my stepfather had a boy, he is my *half-brother*.

4 Poor Aunt Jane. She was *widowed* last year when her husband died, she still misses him.

5 'Do you like your *mother-in-law*?' 'I can't say. Both my wife's parents died before I met her.'

6 Even though we were *divorced* five years ago, I'm still good friends with my *ex-wife*.

7 'Do you ever want to get married?' 'No thanks, I want to stay *single* – it's much more fun!'

(**Note:** The word *stepbrother* is not used.)

Exercise 3

1	Have you got any cousins?	d	Yes, I have. I have two cousins.
2	Is your sister older than you?	b	No, she isn't. She's two years younger.
3	How many brothers and and sisters have you got?	e	I've got one brother and one sister.
4	Are you married?	a	No, I'm not. I'm single.
5	Do you like your brother?	f	No, I don't really like him, although I do like my sister.
6	Who's your [favourite/ favorite] relation?	c	My Aunt Polly. She's great. She's so much fun.

Reading

Reading 1 Mrs. Saunders only has her son, William (she's widowed, and she and William are both only children).

Reading 2

1 Kate's grandmother is the mother of Kate's [mum/mom]. ✔

2 Kate is married. ✗ Kate is **divorced** (she had an ex-husband who's still alive). She's getting married to William in the future.

3 Kate's mother and father are married. ✗ Kate's mother and father are **divorced**.

4 Kate's brother George's new child will have twenty-one cousins. ✔ *(Kate has twelve nephews and nine nieces; they are all cousins.)*

5 Mrs. Saunders is a widower. ✗ Mrs. Saunders is a **widow**.

6 Kate's brothers and sisters are all older than she is, but her half-brother is younger. ✔
7 Kate's stepfather has two sisters. ✗ Kate's stepfather has two **daughters** (they're <u>Kate's</u> stepsisters).
8 William has no father. ✔ *(Mrs. Saunders is widowed.)*
9 Kate's brothers and sisters have had more sons than daughters. ✔ *(Kate has twelve nephews – boys – and only nine nieces – girls.)*
10 Kate's grandmother has eight grandchildren. ✗ Kate's grandmother has **nine** grandchildren (eight brothers and sisters <u>and</u> Kate herself).

Listening

Listening 1

1 Are you married? ✔

2 Have you got any children? ✔

3 Who's your [favourite/favorite] relation? ☐

4 Is your brother older or younger than you? ☐

5 What about your parents, are they still alive? ✔

Listening 2

Name	Marion Jacobs
Marital status	single
Children	no children
Parents	mother (widow – father is dead)
Brothers	one (half-brother)
Sisters	two

10

food (1)

In this chapter you will learn
- the names of many foods
- different types of food and meal times (fruit, snacks, dinner...)
- how to ask for/offer something to eat

Basics

Do you know these words? Check in a dictionary and write the word in your language.

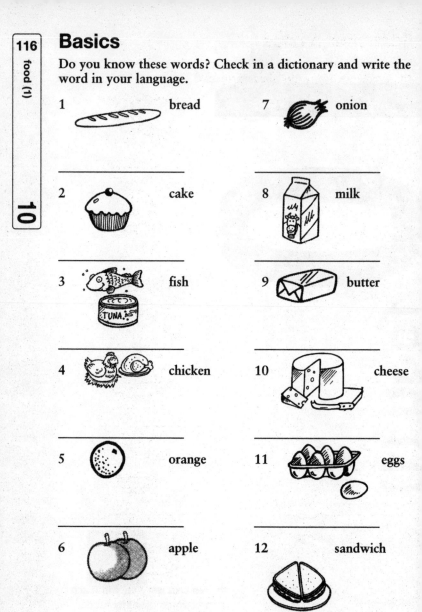

1 bread

2 cake

3 fish

4 chicken

5 orange

6 apple

7 onion

8 milk

9 butter

10 cheese

11 eggs

12 sandwich

Test your basics

Cover the words on page 116 so you can't see them. Then write the English word in the space provided.

1

orange

2

_____

3

_____

4

_____

5

_____

6

_____

7

_____

8

_____

9

_____

10

_____

11

_____

12

_____

Extension

Some types of food

Look at these different types of food. Use the examples from Basics to help you understand the meaning, as well as a dictionary, if you need to.

- **Fruit**, for example apples and oranges.
- **Vegetables**, for example, onions.
- **Meat**, for example, chicken.
- **Dairy**, for example, milk, butter, cheese and eggs.
- [**Sweets/Candy**] are often eaten as a snack and have lots of sugar. **Chocolate** is also popular.
- **Snacks** are light food you eat between meals for example, a sandwich or chocolate could be a snack.

More food

See if you know these different foods; look up any you don't know in a dictionary.

- Fruit: a **banana** is long and yellow; a **pear** is green; a **lemon** is small and yellow.

- Vegetables: **potatoes** come from the ground and are very popular; **peas** are small and green; **carrots** are long, thin, and orange; **salads** make light meals and are popular in summer.

- Meat: **beef** is the meat from cows, **lamb** is the meat from sheep, and **pork** is the meat from pigs. A **steak** is a cooked piece of meat, usually beef.

- Snacks: in Britain, **chips** are made from potatoes and are cooked and eaten hot – Americans call them **French fries**. In Britain, **crisps** are also made from potatoes and come in bags – Americans call these **potato chips**!

- Dairy: **yoghurt** is made from milk and often contains fruit.

- **Rice** is a very popular and important food in Asia; **pasta** (for example, spaghetti) comes from Italy; **sugar** is used in [sweets/candy], but is bad for your teeth; **flour** is used for making bread.

- People often put **salt** and **pepper** on their food and in their cooking for extra taste.

Meals

- A **meal** is when we sit down to eat. We normally use the verb **have** with meals.

- **Breakfast** is the first meal of the day. People often have **toast** (cooked bread) with butter and **jam** (normally made from fruit). **Marmalade** is a special jam made from oranges or lemons. Many people eat **cereal** which you have with milk, for example cornflakes.

- **Lunch** is in the middle of the day. You might have something like **soup** (a hot food that is liquid, often made from vegetables and/or meat).

• **Dinner** is the big evening meal, for example steak with potatoes and vegetables or salad.

Note: In the US *dinner* is often called *supper*, but in Britain supper is a smaller meal which you eat later in the evening.

Questions and phrases

• If you want something to eat, then you feel **hungry** (adjective).
• We can ask **Are you hungry?**
• To ask what someone wants, we use **would like**:
  What would you like (to eat)?
  I'd like...
• We offer food by asking **Would you like something to eat?** Or we can request food by asking **Could I have...?**
• **Do you like...?** asks about general likes and dislikes.
• If you want to know about times of meals, ask **What time do you have ...?**

Examples:

Are you hungry?	Yes, I am./No, I'm not.
I'm hungry.	OK, what would you like to eat?
I'd like an apple, please.	Certainly, here you are./I'm sorry, I haven't got any. Would you like an orange instead?
What would you like (to eat)?	I'd like a sandwich, please.
Would you like something to eat?	Yes, could I have a cake, please?/No thanks, I'm not hungry.
Could I have some cheese, please?	No problem, here you are./I'm sorry, I don't have any cheese.
Do you like yoghurt?	Yes, I do./No, I don't.
What time do you have dinner?	At seven o'clock.

Practice

Exercise 1 Make the correct food from these anagrams. Then put them into the table. There are three words for each part of the table.

1 geg *egg*	6 meoln	11 clunh
2 ebef	7 esehec	12 cneikhc
3 daals	8 pepurs	13 sepa
4 abml	9 totapo	14 rubtet
5 rekabstaf	10 repa	15 anaban

dairy	fruit	vegetable	meat	meal
egg				

Exercise 2 Fill the gaps with the correct word from the box below. One word is *not* used.

1 Would you like some __*milk*__ for your cereal?

2 What would you like to _____?

3 'I always have orange _____ on my toast.' 'Really? I prefer _____.'

4 The _____ in [sweets/candy] is bad for your teeth.

5 In America they use the words _____ for crisps.

6 I love dairy foods like cheese and _____.

7 What time is _____? I'm really hungry.

8 I was late this morning, so I didn't _____ any breakfast.

> potato chips   dinner   eat   French fries   have
> jam   marmalade   ~~milk~~   sugar   yoghurt

Exercise 3 Match the correct sentence or question with its response.

1 What time do you have breakfast?	No, I'm not. How about you?
2 Do you like chicken?	Quite late, at eight o'clock.
3 What would you like to eat for lunch?	Of course. Would you like an apple, a pear, or an orange?
4 Would you like something to eat?	Could I have some soup, please?
5 I'm hungry.	No thanks, I'm not hungry at the moment.
6 Could I have some fruit, please?	OK, what would you like in it? Cheese? Jam?
7 Are you hungry?	No, I don't. I don't like any meat.
8 I'd like a sandwich, please.	OK, would you like a sandwich?

Now check your answers.

▶ **Exercise 4 (Recordings 10.1, 10.2, 10.3, 10.4, 10.5)** Pronunciation practice. Listen and repeat the words on the recording. Use the transcript at the back to help you if necessary.

In use

Reading

Before you start, check you know these words:

> doctor   iron   protein   digestion   bones   obesity

Note: *'Greens'* is another way of saying vegetables like *cabbage* or *spinach* or other green vegetables. *Fat* is not good for you – there's a lot of fat in meat but none in fruit and vegetables.

You are going to read a magazine article about healthy eating.

Reading 1 Read the article and put the headings from the box into the right places.

Cereals   Dairy products   Fruit and vegetables   Meat   Snacks

Eat your way to health!

What you eat can say a lot about how long you live...

1 *Fruit and vegetables*

In the Western world we don't eat anything like enough. Try to eat your greens, they really are one of the best foods for you. *An apple a day keeps the doctor away*, but make sure you eat some oranges, bananas, carrots and salad too!

2 _____

It's not always bad for you. Beef, pork, lamb – they're all good sources of iron and protein. But don't eat too much (and most people in the Western world do) – no more than once a day. Or eat less red meat and more white, for example, chicken, which really is much better for you.

3 _____

We don't have enough of these either in the West, but again, they really are very good for you, particularly your digestion. So eat lots of bread and try to have a bowl of cereal for breakfast.

4 _____

Very good for building strong bones, foods like milk, cheese and yoghurt are very important, particularly for children. And if you're worried about obesity, then there are lots of low fat varieties available too (but young children should never eat low fat foods, they need full fat).

5 _____

We all love them, but things like [crisps/potato chips] and chocolate really are not doing your body any good. Try to have an apple instead. Not only is it better for you, it tastes better too!

Reading 2 Decide if the following statements are true (✔) or false (✗), then correct the ones that are false.

1 Fruit and vegetables are good for your health. ✔
2 Have a bowl of cereal for dinner. ✗ Have a bowl of cereal for breakfast.
3 Apples taste better than [crisps/potato chips].
4 Meat is always bad for you.
5 Cheese is good for the bones.
6 People say 'an orange a day keeps the doctor away'.
7 Young children should have low fat dairy foods.
8 Chicken is a kind of red meat.
9 Cereals are good for your digestion.
10 [Crisps/potato chips] and chocolate are bad for you.

▶ Listening

Before you start, check you know these words:

survey	soon	nothing (else)

You will hear three short conversations involving food.

Listening 1 (Recording 10.6) For each conversation there are two questions below. Listen to the recording and put a ✔ next to the question you hear.

1 (A) Would you like some beef?
  (B) Do you like beef?

2 (A) Do you have breakfast?
  (B) What would you like for breakfast?

3 (A) Could I have a sandwich?
  (B) Would you like a sandwich?

Listening 2 Listen to the recording again and write down all the foods you hear. There are seven foods in total.

Now check your answers.

Recap

Here are the words we learned in this unit. Do you know them all? Write down the translations if necessary.

Types of food

fruit	vegetable	meat
dairy	snack	[sweets/candy]

Fruit and vegetables

orange	apple	banana
pear	lemon	onion
potato	peas	carrot
salad		

Meat

fish	chicken	beef
lamb	pork	steak

Dairy

milk	butter	cheese
egg	yoghurt	

Snacks

sandwich	[crisps/potato chips]	[chips/French fries]
chocolate		

Meals and other foods

have a meal	breakfast	lunch
dinner	supper	toast
jam	marmalade	cereal
soup	rice	pasta
sugar	flour	salt
pepper		

Questions and phrases

Are you hungry?   I'm hungry.
What would you like (to eat)?   I'd like an apple, please.
Would you like something to eat?
Could I have some cheese, please?
Do you like yoghurt?
What time do you have dinner?

What to do next

• Find the English word for any food that you eat that isn't in this unit and write it down.
• Tell someone about the foods you like and don't like.
• See if you can read anything about food in English; see how many foods you know.

Why not try this unit next?

• Food (2)

Answer key for this unit

Test your basics

1 orange

2 milk

3 chicken

4 onion

5 egg

6 bread

7	apple

10	sandwich

8	fish

11	cake

9	cheese

12	butter

Exercise 1

1 egg	6 lemon	11 lunch
2 beef	7 cheese	12 chicken
3 salad	8 supper	13 peas
4 lamb	9 potato	14 butter
5 breakfast	10 pear	15 banana

dairy	fruit	vegetable	meat	meal
egg	lemon	salad	beef	breakfast
cheese	pear	potato	lamb	supper
butter	banana	peas	chicken	lunch

Exercise 2

1 Would you like some *milk* for your cereal?
2 What would you like to *eat*?
3 'I always have orange *marmalade* on my toast.' 'Really? I prefer *jam*.'
4 The *sugar* in [sweets/candy] is bad for your teeth.
5 In America they use the words *potato chips* for crisps.
6 I love dairy foods like cheese and *yoghurt*.
7 What time is *dinner*? I'm really hungry.
8 I was late this morning, so I didn't *have* any breakfast.
(*French fries* is not used.)

Exercise 3

1 What time do you have breakfast?	Quite late, at eight o'clock.
2 Do you like chicken?	No, I don't. I don't like any meat.
3 What would you like to eat for lunch?	Could I have some soup, please?
4 Would you like something to eat?	No thanks. I'm not hungry at the moment.
5 I'm hungry.	OK, would you like a sandwich?
6 Could I have some fruit, please?	Of course. Would you like an apple, a pear, or an orange?
7 Are you hungry?	No, I'm not. How about you?
8 I'd like a sandwich, please.	OK, what would you like in it? Cheese? Jam?

Reading

Reading 1

1 Fruit and vegetables 2 Meat 3 Cereals 4 Dairy products 5 Snacks

Reading 2

1 Fruit and vegetables are good for your health. ✔
2 Have a bowl of cereal for dinner. ✘ Have a bowl of cereal for **breakfast**.
3 Apples taste better than [crisps/potato chips]. ✔
4 Meat is always bad for you. ✘ Some meat is **good** for you – it's good for iron and protein.
5 Cheese is good for the bones. ✔
6 People say an orange a day keeps the doctor away. ✘ People say an **apple** a day keeps the doctor away.
7 Young children should have low fat dairy foods. ✘ Young children should **never** have low fat dairy foods; they should have full fat.
8 Chicken is a kind of red meat. ✘ Chicken is a kind of **white** meat.
9 Cereals are good for your digestion. ✔
10 [Crisps/potato chips] and chocolate are bad for you. ✔

Listening

Listening 1

1 (A) ~~Would you like some beef?~~
   (B) Do you like beef? ✔

2 (A) Do you have breakfast? ✔
   (B) ~~What would you like for breakfast?~~

3 (A) Could I have a sandwich? ✔
   (B) ~~Would you like a sandwich?~~

Listening 2

The seven foods are:

(roast) beef, (roast) potatoes (Conversation 1)
toast, jam, marmalade (Conversation 2)
sandwich, potato chips (Conversation 3)

food (2)

In this unit you will learn
- words for ways of cooking/preparing food
- words for equipment used when making/preparing food
- how to order food in a restaurant

Basics

Make sure you know all the words from Food (1) before you do
this unit! Do you know these words? Check in a dictionary and
write the word in your language.

1 oven

6 microwave

2 [grill/broiler]

7 [jug/pitcher]

3 [hob/burner]

8 knife

4  saucepan

9 fork

5  frying pan

10 spoon

Test your basics

Write the English words in the space below. Don't look at page 131!

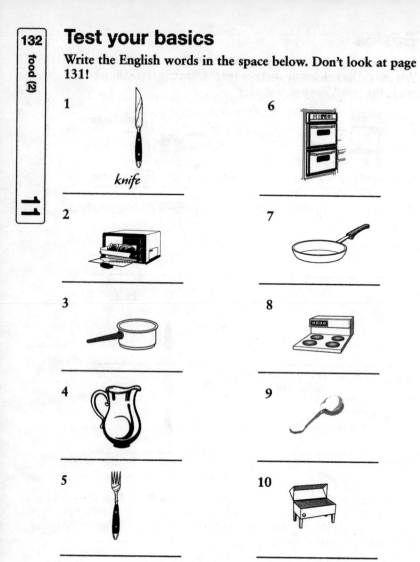

1 *knife*

2

3

4

5

6

7

8

9

10

Extension

Ways of cooking (verbs and adjectives)

- We often use **oil** for cooking; with oil we can **fry** food (adjective = **fried**), for example potatoes.
- We can also use water to cook with in a saucepan; if we heat the water to 100°C (212°F), we **boil** it (adjective = **boiled**), for example, boiled potatoes.
- If the water is a little cooler, then we use the verb **simmer**, for example, we simmer a sauce.
- We [**grill/broil**] food under the [grill/broiler] (adjective = [**grilled/broiled**]).
- We **bake** food in the oven (adjective = **baked**), for example bread.
- When we cook food in an oven with oil or **fat**, we use the verb **roast** (adjective = **roast**), for example, roast beef.
- Food that is not cooked is **raw**, for example, raw fish.
- We can **freeze** food (adjective = **frozen**) – that is, make it very cold by putting it in the **freezer**, for example, ice cream.

Equipment and preparation

- With a [jug/pitcher] we can **measure** liquids; for solids we use [**scales/measuring cups**].
- When you **pour** something out of a [jug/pitcher], you empty it.
- When you put two or more foods together, you **mix** them. For example, you mix sugar, butter, and flour to make a cake.
- With a spoon you can **stir**; with a knife you can **cut**. If we cut something many times or without much care, we often use the verb **chop**; for example, you cut a cake but you chop carrots.
- Before cooking with eggs we often **beat** them.
- We often **add** a little salt and pepper for taste, and when food is ready we **serve** it.
- To measure liquids we use [**litres/liters**] or **pints** [1 UK pint = 0.56 litres/1 US pint = 0.47 litres].
- For weights we use **kilograms** or **pounds** (1kg = 2.2 pounds).

Nouns and adjectives

- **Ingredients** are what we use to make something. For example, flour, eggs, milk, and sugar are the ingredients of cake.
- A **recipe** is the list of instructions which tells us how to make something.

Look at these opposites:

- Food can be **hot** or **cold**; 'hot food' can also mean **spicy**, for example, **curry** (a meat or vegetable dish that comes from India). The opposite of spicy is **mild**.
- **Sweet** food has lots of sugar, for example, chocolate. The opposite is **bitter** or **sour**.
- [**Savoury/savory**] food does not contain a lot of sugar. It can be **salty** or spicy.
- Food you really like is **delicious**. Food that has no taste or [**flavour/flavor**] is **tasteless**. The opposite of tasteless is **tasty**.

Ordering food

- You order food in a restaurant from a **waiter** or a **waitress**.

Look at the example conversation below:

Waiter	Customer
Are you ready to order?	Yes, please./Could you give us some more time, please?
What would you like?	I'd like...
And for you, sir/[madam/ma'am]?	Could I have... please?

Questions and sentences

- To ask what someone thinks of their food we can say **What's your... like?**
- To ask for a recipe we can ask **How do you make...?**
- To give a recipe we can use joining words like **First... Then... Next... Finally...**

Examples:

What's your pizza like?

It's delicious./It's cold and tasteless.

How do you make an [omelette/omlet]?

First you take two eggs. Then you beat them with some milk and add salt and pepper. Next you cook it in a frying pan and finally serve it with some salad.

Practice

Exercise 1 See if you can do this crossword.

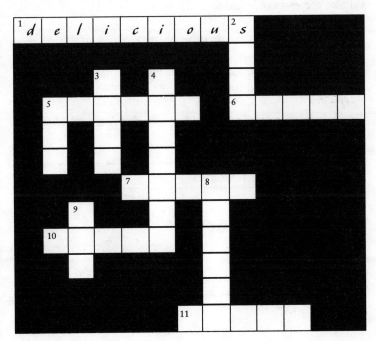

Across

1 Opposite of tasteless

5 Ice cream must be...
6 A way of cooking meat in the oven
7 A famous food from India
10 A measure, for example of milk (British spelling)
11 After you've made something, you _____ it

Down

2 Opposite of sweet
3 A way of cooking using very hot water
4 You can use a [jug/pitcher] to _____ liquids
5 A way of cooking, for example for steak
8 The instructions for cooking something
9 You need this to do no. 5 down and no. 6!

Exercise 2 Put the sentences below into the correct order to make the conversation between a waiter and two customers.

What would you like, [madam/ma'am]?

I'd like the chicken, please.

Yes, we are, please.

And could we have a bottle of wine, please?

I'd like the steak, please.

Of course, [madam/ma'am]. Red or white?

Steak. Certainly. And for you, sir?

Yes, sir.

Good evening, sir. Good evening, [madam/ma'am]. Are you ready to order?

Waiter	Woman	Man
1	2	
3	4	
5		6
7	8	
9		

Exercise 3 Fill in the missing words from the box for this recipe for fruit cake. One of the words is *not* used.

Note: *Raisins* are a kind of fruit made from dried grapes; a *cake tin* is used for making cakes.

To make fruit cake you need 240g flour, 240g butter, 160g sugar, a little milk, some raisins, and one egg. First 1 __*mix*__ the flour and butter together, then 2 _____ the egg and 3 _____ it to the sugar and raisins. 4 _____ in some milk, and 5 _____ everything together. 6 _____ put the mixture into the cake tin using a clean 7 _____. 8 _____ put the cake tin into a cool 9 _____ and 10 _____ for one hour, ten minutes. 11 _____ hot.

add	bake	beat	finally	~~mix~~	next
oven	pour	roast	serve	spoon	stir

Now check your answers.

▶ **Exercise 4 (Recordings 11.1, 11.2, 11.3, 11.4, 11.5)** Pronunciation practice. Listen and repeat the words on the recording. Use the transcript at the back of the book to help you if necessary.

In use

Reading

Before you start, check you know these words:

foreign country   stomach   silent   burnt   honest   disgusting

Note: *Lines* are the words an actor has to learn; *to leave it to the last minute* is to do something as late as possible.

You Can't Do It Again, My Son is British actor Steven Quinn's story of his life. Here he talks about a time when he did some cooking for a girlfriend.

Reading 1 What did his guest think of his meal?

To me the kitchen was like a foreign country, and one that I didn't want to visit. But I had promised, so I had to do it. And anyway, how difficult was roast chicken? I had a few vegetables – peas, carrots, potatoes. It was all looking good. I knew that Belinda really liked hot food, like curry, but my British stomach preferred something milder.

My first shock was when I found out I couldn't just put it in the microwave. The recipe book said use an oven, for two hours! I always leave my lines to the last minute, but suddenly I realized this wasn't a very good idea with a recipe. Never mind, I thought. Just make the oven hotter and the food will cook faster.

Finally Belinda came around and I put the meal before her. We ate and quickly went silent. The chicken was hot and burnt on the outside and cold on the inside, while my vegetables were nearly raw. I looked at my guest.

'Well, what do you think?' I tried. She looked at me and smiled before putting down her knife and fork.

'Absolutely disgusting,' Belinda said. Well, she was certainly honest!

Reading 2 Answer the following questions.

1 Did Steven often go into his kitchen?

   No. It was like a foreign country.

2 What was Steven going to cook?
3 What kind of food did Belinda like?
4 Where did Steven want to cook his roast chicken?
5 How did Steven think you could make food cook faster?
6 Were the vegetables cooked a lot or a little? How do you know?
7 What did Belinda do before she spoke to Steven?

► Listening

Before you start, check you know these words:

> vanilla extract   dish (to cook in)   bowl   cream

Note: We cut bread into *slices*; there are sixteen *ounces* in a pound; 190°C (*400°F*) is a temperature.

You're going to hear a recipe on a radio show.

Listening 1 (Recording 11.6) Listen to the first section *only* and complete the list of ingredients below.

four slices of white _____
some _____
some raisins
120g of _____
_____ eggs
half a pint (a quarter of a [litre/liter]) of _____
vanilla extract

Listening 2 Listen now to the second section of the recording and put the recipe into the correct order.

Put the bread in a dish and add the raisins and sugar. ☐
Beat the eggs in a bowl and stir in the milk and vanilla extract. ☐
Make two sandwiches from the bread. ☐
Pour the eggs, milk and vanilla extract over the bread. ☐
Spread the butter on the bread. [1]
Put in a hot oven (190°C/400°F) for 35–40 minutes. ☐
Cut each sandwich into six pieces. ☐
Serve hot with cream. ☐
Leave for 15 minutes. ☐

Now check your answers.

Recap

Here are the words we learned in this unit. Do you know them all? Write down the translations if you need to.

Equipment

oven	[grill/broiler]	[hob/burner]
saucepan	frying pan	microwave
[jug/pitcher]	knife	fork
spoon	[scales/measuring cups]	

Preparing food

measure	pour	mix
stir	cut	chop
beat	add	serve
[litre/liter]	pint	kilogram
pound		

Ways of cooking

oil	fat	fry (fried)
boil (boiled)	simmer	[grill (grilled)/broil (broiled)]
bake (baked)	roast (roast)	
raw	freeze (frozen)	

Nouns and adjectives

ingredients	recipe	curry
hot	cold	spicy
mild	sweet	sour
bitter	[savoury/savory]	salty
delicious	tasteless	tasty

Questions and phrases

What's your... like? How do you make? First... Then...
Next... Finally...

Ordering food

Are you ready to order?	Yes, please.
Could you give us a little more time, please?	What would you like?
And for you, sir /[madam/ma'am]?	I'd like...
Could I have... please?	

What to do next

- Imagine you are in a restaurant. Try ordering your [favourite/favorite] meal.
- Write down your [favourite/favorite] recipe and try it out on a friend.
- See if you can find any other recipes in English and try them.

Why not try these units next?

- Drink • Shopping

Answer key for this unit

Test your basics

1 knife

5 fork

2 microwave

6 oven

3 saucepan

7 frying pan

4 [jug/pitcher]

8 hob

9 spoon

10 [grill/broiler]

Exercise 1

¹d	e	l	i	c	i	o	u	²s		
								o		
			³b		⁴m			u		
	⁵f	r	o	z	e	n		⁶r	o	a	s	t
	r		i		a					
	y		l		s					
				⁷c	u	r	⁸r	y		
		⁹o			r		e			
¹⁰l	i	t	r	e			c			
	l						i			
							p			
				¹¹s	e	r	v	e		

Exercise 2

Waiter	Woman	Man
1 Good evening, sir, good evening, [madam/ma'am]. Are you ready to order?	2 Yes, we are, please.	
3 What would you like, [madam/ma'am]?	4 I'd like the steak, please.	

Waiter	Woman	Man
5 Steak. Certainly. And for you, sir?		6 I'd like the chicken, please.
7 Yes, sir.	8 And could we have a bottle of wine, please?	
9 Of course, [madam/ma'am]. Red or white?		

Exercise 3

To make fruit cake you need 240g flour, 240g butter, 160g sugar, a little milk, some raisins, and one egg. First **1** *mix* the flour and butter together, then **2** *beat* the egg and **3** *add* it to the sugar and raisins. **4** *Pour* in some milk, and **5** *stir* everything together. **6** *Next* put the mixture into the cake tin using a clean **7** *spoon*. **8** *Finally* put the cake tin into a cool **9** *oven* and **10** *bake* for one hour, ten minutes. **11** *Serve* hot.

(*roast* is not used)

Reading

Reading 1

Belinda thought the meal was absolutely disgusting.

Reading 2

1 No. It was like a foreign country.
2 He was going to cook roast chicken with peas, carrots, and potatoes.
3 She liked hot, spicy food (for example, curry).
4 He wanted to cook it in the microwave.
5 By making the oven hotter.
6 They were cooked a little (they were nearly raw).
7 She put down her knife and fork.

Listening

Listening 1

four slices of white *bread*
some *butter*
some raisins
120g of *sugar*
two eggs
half a pint (a quarter of a [litre/liter]) of *milk*
vanilla extract

Listening 2

Put the bread in a dish and add the raisins and sugar. ⎢4⎢

Beat the eggs in a bowl and stir in the milk and vanilla extract. ⎢5⎢

Make two sandwiches from the bread. ⎢2⎢

Pour the eggs, milk and vanilla extract over the bread. ⎢6⎢

Spread the butter on the bread. ⎢1⎢

Put in a hot oven (190°C/400°F) for 35–40 minutes. ⎢8⎢

Cut each sandwich into six pieces. ⎢3⎢

Serve hot with cream. ⎢9⎢

Leave for 15 minutes. ⎢7⎢

12

house and household (1)

In this unit you will learn
- the names of places to live (house, flat...)
- words for size/style/rooms
- how to ask questions about/describe your home (How many rooms has it got? It's got a small kitchen...)

Basics

Do you know these words? Check in a dictionary and write the word in your language.

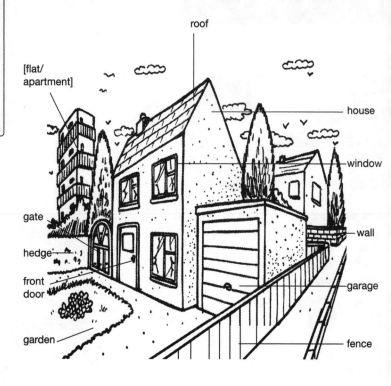

roof

[flat/apartment]

house

window

gate

wall

hedge

front door

garage

garden

fence

Note: *household* can be a noun or an adjective. When it is a noun, it means 'family' or 'house'. When it is an adjective, it means 'relating to a house', for example, 'household objects' = things in a house.

Test your basics

Cover the words on page 146 so you can't see them. Then write the English words below.

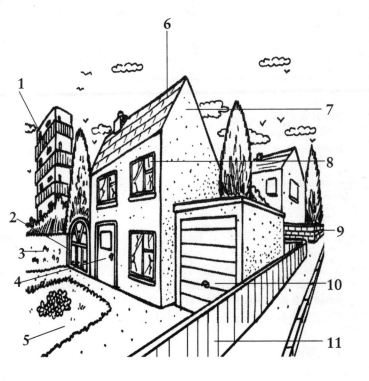

Extension

Rooms and garden

- **Room** is the general word for space in a house.

- Houses usually have two **floors**; **upstairs** and **downstairs**.

- Downstairs most houses have a **kitchen** where you prepare food; a **dining room** where you eat; a **living room** where you relax and perhaps watch television and a **hall** where you enter the house. Some houses have a downstairs **toilet**.

Note: In the US the toilet is also often called the **bathroom**.

- Some houses also have a **basement** or **cellar** under the house.

- Upstairs you usually have **bedrooms** to sleep in and a **bathroom** for washing. Many houses also have a **study** for people to work in.

- A lot of houses also have an **attic** (or **loft**) which is under the roof.

Gardens

- Most houses have a **front** [garden/yard] and a **back** [garden/yard].

- [Gardens/yards] often have a **lawn** (an area of grass); they sometimes have a **driveway** for the car and, in the back, a **patio** (an area without grass).

- They also have **flowers, trees,** hedges and fences.

Adjectives

Look at these opposites:

- A house, [flat/apartment], or room … can be **big, large** or **small**; it can be **bright** or **dark**; it can be **warm** or **cold**; it can be **old** or **new** and its style can be **traditional** or **modern**; it can also be **beautiful** or **ugly**.

Examples:

Our house is very large.

We have a modern [flat/apartment].

The dining room is quite dark.

Our house is ugly, but the garden is beautiful.

- You might have one room you like more than others – this is your [**favourite/favorite**].

  Examples:

  My [favourite/favorite] room is the kitchen. It's very warm.

  My [favourite/favorite] part of the house is the [garden/yard]. It has lots of flowers and a big lawn.

Note: We normally put the [colour/color] just before the noun. For example: a small white kitchen, a traditional blue dining room.

Questions and sentences

- We can use [**have got/have**] to talk about possession – number of rooms, garden, etc. Be careful with the grammar and the negative forms of each, for example:

  Our [flat/apartment] has got a beautiful, green bathroom, but it hasn't got a downstairs toilet.

  Our house has a small back [garden/yard], but it doesn't have a front [garden/yard].

General questions

- **Where do you live?**
- **How many rooms has... got?** or **How many rooms does... have?**
- For something specific, we can ask **Has your... got a ...?** or **Does your... have a ...?**
- **What [colour/color] is your...?**
- We can use the question **What's your... like?** to ask about everything.

  Examples:

Where do you live?	In a small [flat/apartment].
How many rooms has your [flat/apartment] got?	It's got five rooms.
What [colour/color] is your living room?	It's orange.

| Does your house have a [garden/yard]? | Yes, it has./No, it hasn't. |
| What's your kitchen like? | It's quite small and dark. |

Practice

Exercise 1 Complete the crossword with the correct rooms.

Across

1 The room where you do the cooking
3 Also known as the basement
5 The room where you wash yourself
7 The room where you eat
8 Another word for attic
9 A room to work in

Down

2 Where you enter the house
4 Most people watch TV in the living...
5 You sleep in here
6 It's useful to have a downstairs...

Exercise 2 Look at the answers below and write the question.

1 How many rooms has your flat got? *or* How many rooms does your house have?
It['s got/has] six rooms – a kitchen, a living room, a bathroom and three bedrooms.

2 _____ ?
It's beautiful, with lots of flowers and a big lawn.

3 _____ ?
We live in a modern [flat/apartment].

4 _____ ?
Our bedroom is only small, but it's really warm in winter.

5 _____ ?
Yes it has. It['s got/has] a big garden with a small patio.

6 _____ ?
Our bathroom is blue.

7 _____ ?
It's quite old. It['s got/has] a small front garden; it [hasn't got/doesn't have] a garage, but it['s got/has] a driveway and it['s got/has] three bedrooms.

Exercise 3 For each question in this exercise, replace the underlined word with its opposite.

1 We have a large (*small*) front [garden/yard].
2 Your living room is so dark (*bright*).
3 This is quite a cold (   ) room.
4 We don't have a front (   ) [garden/yard].
5 I really like traditional (   ) houses.
6 The bathroom is downstairs (   ).
7 Their house is really ugly (   ).
8 You always get problems with new (   ) houses.

Now check your answers.

▶ **Exercise 4 (Recordings 12.1, 12.2, 12.3, 12.4)** Pronunciation practice. Listen and repeat the words on the recording. Use the transcript at the back of the book to help you if necessary.

In use

Reading

Before you start, check you know these words:

decorate   owner   balcony   (good) condition

Note: An [*estate agent/realtor*] is someone who sells houses. *Brand new* means very new.

Reading Read the descriptions of three houses below and complete the notes underneath. The first one has been done to help you.

McAllister & Sons, Estate Agents

1 17 Mandarin Gardens

This modern 1970s house is quite near the city [centre/center] and is close to many [shops/stores]. It has a living room, a dining room, and a kitchen downstairs and three bedrooms and a bathroom upstairs. It is quite small, but has a large [back garden/ backyard] with a small patio. It also has a garage. The rooms are bright and warm and it is in good condition.

2 10 Clifton Court

Large three bedroom [flat/apartment] situated on the third floor. Brand new and ready for first owners, this [flat/apartment] has a bathroom, a living room and a large kitchen with plenty of space to eat in. Decorated in a very modern style it also has a garage. The [flat/apartment] has a large balcony.

3 42 Morley Road

Beautiful, old four-bedroom house. This house has three large bedrooms and one smaller bedroom, which would be perfect for a study. The [back garden/backyard] is small, but has lots of flowers and is in good condition. It also has a living room, dining room, kitchen, downstairs toilet, and bathroom upstairs. There is a cellar and a large attic. The house is in need of some repainting.

1 17 Mandarin Gardens

bedrooms	3	house	*quite modern*
bathroom	*yes* (upstairs)	garden	*yes (large back [garden/yard], small patio)*
living room	*yes*		
dining room	*yes*	garage	*yes*
kitchen	*yes*	attic	*no*
extra toilet	*no*	cellar	*no*

2 10 Clifton Court

bedrooms		house	
bathroom		garden	
living room		garage	
dining room		attic	
kitchen		cellar	
extra toilet			

3 42 Morley Road

bedrooms		house	
bathroom		garden	
living room		garage	
dining room		attic	
kitchen		cellar	
extra toilet			

▶ Listening

Steve and Cath have two boys and one girl and are buying a house, but are short of money. They have seen the three places in the reading exercise above. Which one do you think is best for them? Why?

Listening 1 (Recording 12.5) Listen to Steve and Cath. Which house do they decide to buy?

Listening 2 Listen to the recording again and match the description to the correct house by putting 1 for Mandarin Gardens, 2 for Clifton Court or 3 for Morley Road. Be careful – one of the descriptions is *not* used.

	Old garage
	A horrible green bedroom
	Warm bedrooms
	A small bathroom
	Cath's [favourite/favorite] garden
	Small windows
	A bright living room
3	A really ugly house

Now check your answers.

Recap

Here are the words we learned in this unit. Do you know them all? Write down the translations if necessary.

Nouns

house	roof	[garden/yard]
garage	gate	[flat/apartment]
front door	hedge	fence
window	wall	household

Rooms and garden

room	floor	upstairs
downstairs	kitchen	dining room
living room	hall	toilet
basement (cellar)	bedroom	bathroom
study	attic (loft)	[front, back garden/ front, backyard]
lawn	patio	driveway
flowers	trees	

Adjectives

household	big	large
small	bright	dark
warm	cold	old
new	traditional	modern
beautiful	ugly	

Questions and sentences

Our... [has got/has] ...	Where do you live?
How many rooms does... have? got?	How many room has...
Does your... have a...?	Has your... got a...?
What's your... like?	

What to do next

- Describe your house to a friend out loud or in a letter.
- Look at pictures of houses – can you describe them?
- See if you can find any descriptions of houses in newspapers, magazines or books.

Why not try this unit next?

- House and household (2)

Answer key for this unit

Test your basics

Look at Basics on page 146 to check your answers.

Exercise 1

Exercise 2

1 How many rooms has your house got? *or* How many rooms does your house have?
2 What's your [garden/yard] like?
3 Where do you live?
4 What's your bedroom like?
5 Has your house got a [back garden/backyard]? *or* Does your house have a [back garden/backyard]?
6 What [colour/color] is your bathroom?
7 What's your house like?

Exercise 3

1 We have a *small* front [garden/yard].
2 Your living room is so *bright*.
3 This is quite a *warm* room.
4 We don't have a *back* [garden/yard].
5 I really like *modern* houses.
6 The bathroom is *upstairs*.
7 Their house is really *beautiful*.
8 You always get problems with *old* houses.

Reading

Reading

1 17 Mandarin Gardens

bedrooms	3	house	*quite modern*
bathroom	*yes (upstairs)*	garden	*yes (large back [garden/yard], small patio)*
living room	*yes*		
dining room	*yes*	garage	*yes*
kitchen	*yes*	attic	*no*
extra toilet	*no*	cellar	*no*

2 10 Clifton Court

bedrooms	3	house	brand new flat
bathroom	yes	garden	no (balcony)
living room	yes	garage	yes
dining room	no	attic	no
kitchen	yes	cellar	no
extra toilet	no		

3 42 Morley Road

bedrooms	4	house	old house
bathroom	yes (upstairs)	garden	yes (small back [garden/yard], lots of flowers)
living room	yes		
dining room	yes	garage	no
kitchen	yes	attic	yes
extra toilet	yes (downstairs)	cellar	yes

Listening

Listening 1

They decide to buy 42 Morley Road.

Listening 2

1	Old garage	2	A bright living room
3	A horrible green bedroom	3	A really ugly house
2	Warm bedrooms		
✗	~~A small bathroom~~		
1	Cath's [favourite/favorite] garden		
1	Small windows		

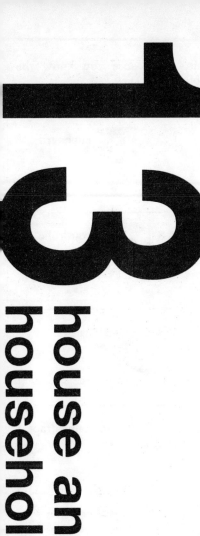

13 house and household (2)

In this unit you will learn
- words for furniture and furnishings (sofa, carpet...)
- how to use prepositions to describe place (next to, near...)
- how to describe what's in a room (Have you got a TV? The bed is next to the window...)

Basics

Note: Before doing this unit, make sure you know the vocabulary from House and household (1).

Do you know these words? Check in a dictionary and write the word in your language.

1 table

7 cupboard

2 chair

8 wardrobe

3 sofa

9  carpet

4 armchair

10 [curtains/drapes]

5 chest of drawers

11 lamp

6 bed

12 light

Test your basics

Cover the words on page 160 so you can't see them. Then write the English words in the spaces below.

1

bed

2

3

4

5

6

7

8

9

10

11

12

Extension

More furniture and furnishings

- **Furniture** is large items in the house, for example a chair or a bed; **furnishings** are small items, for example a lamp.

In the living room

- People often watch a **television** (**TV**) here or a [**video/VCR**], there is also often a **hi-fi** to listen to.
- There might be a **fire** to make the room warm in winter.
- For decoration, there could be **pictures** up on the wall, or perhaps a **plant** or flowers – we normally keep flowers in a **vase**.

In the kitchen

- A **fridge** keeps food (like milk or butter) cold; a **freezer** is colder and lets you keep food for a long time.
- You cook with a [**cooker/stove**] and use a **washing machine** to wash your clothes.
- You eat off **plates** or out of **bowls** using a **knife, fork**, and **spoon**.
- We drink hot drinks from a **cup** and cold drinks from a **glass**.
- You can wash plates etc. by hand in the **sink,** or you can use a machine called a **dishwasher**.

In the bathroom

- Some people like a **bath,** but others prefer a **shower**.
- You wash your hands in a [**basin/sink**] and dry them on a **towel**.
- Many bathrooms also have a **toilet**.

In the bedroom

- There is usually a **mirror** so you can see how you look.
- On the bed we have **sheets, pillows** for our head, and a **blanket** or perhaps a **quilt** to keep warm.
- Some people also have a small piece of furniture called a **bedside cabinet** or **table** next to the bed where they keep things like books etc.

Adjectives and prepositions

- If a bed or a chair is **comfortable**, then it is nice to lie on or sit in; the opposite is **uncomfortable**.
- If something is **heavy**, you need to be strong to pick it up; the opposite is **light**.

Prepositions

Look at the pictures to see how we use these prepositions:

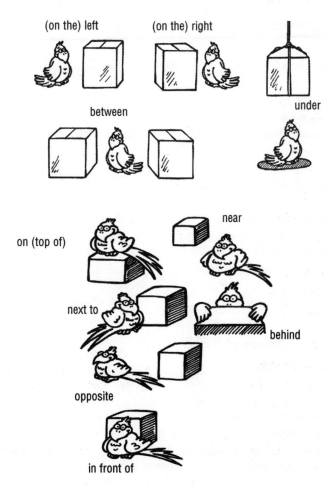

(on the) left

(on the) right

under

between

on (top of)

near

next to

behind

opposite

in front of

Verbs and questions

- To describe a room we often use **there is/are...** or **it [has got/has...]**, for example:

  There's a chair next to the table.

  There are some plates in the dishwasher.

  Our living room [has got/has] a big sofa.

  We have some plants in the kitchen.

Questions

- **Is there a...** *or* **Are there any... in your...** (room)?
- To ask what is in a particular room, we can ask **What's in your...?**
- To ask the location of a room or a piece of furniture, we can use **Where's your...?**
- **What's your... like?** asks for information about a room in general.

  Examples:

Have you got a dishwasher?	Yes, we have./No, we haven't.
Is there a TV in your bedroom?	Yes, there is./No, there isn't.
Are there any plants in your house?	Yes, there are./No, there aren't.
What's in your bathroom?	A toilet, a [basin/sink] and a shower.
Where's your washing machine?	In the kitchen, next to the dishwasher.
What's your living room like?	It's quite small. It['s got/has] a sofa and two armchairs and a small table with a TV on it.

Practice

Exercise 1 In the square on the next page there are twelve words, three from each of the rooms in the box below. Find the words then write them under the correct room.

S	G	U	T	O	W	E	L	X	U	E	L	V	N
P	D	I	T	W	N	L	P	H	I	F	E	V	B
O	A	S	D	U	N	D	L	M	R	S	O	F	A
O	J	T	M	E	B	O	W	L	O	C	T	S	D
N	N	T	E	J	O	W	V	B	I	S	R	T	D
Y	P	E	P	P	I	L	L	O	W	B	E	O	I
W	V	L	S	A	G	S	K	L	I	N	E	I	P
S	R	E	D	F	R	E	E	Z	E	R	R	L	N
S	O	V	Z	N	E	J	O	P	C	S	N	E	W
H	L	I	O	U	S	B	R	I	B	N	A	T	D
E	B	S	H	O	W	E	R	L	E	C	O	G	T
E	F	I	C	J	E	C	N	Q	D	T	I	H	S
T	O	O	B	I	A	R	M	C	H	A	I	R	E
H	R	N	M	D	Q	V	P	R	I	A	V	S	L

bathroom	bedroom	living room	kitchen
			spoon

Exercise 2 Match the first half of the following sentences with its end. One ending is *not* used.

1 The [video/VCR] is under...

2 The plates are in...

3 The bed is between...

4 The towel is next to...

5 The [curtain/drape] is in front of...

6 The quilt is on...

7 The freezer is on the left of...

8 The picture is on...

9 There's a plant on...

the [wardrobe/closet] and the window.

the bed.

the vase.

the TV.

the wall.

the [basin/sink].

the kitchen cupboard.

the table.

the window.

the fridge.

Exercise 3 Put the questions in the correct word order, then match them to the answers. Be careful; one question is *not* used.

1 the hi-fi where's?
Where's the hi-fi?

2 got a you television have?
_____

3 cupboard this what's in?
_____

4 table living a there room is your in?
_____

5 like living your what's room?
_____

a It's quite big. We've got two armchairs and a great big comfortable sofa to sit on.

b Yes, we have. And we've got a [video/VCR] too.

c It's on the chest of drawers, behind the sofa.

d Oh, just some plates, bowls, knives, forks, and spoons.

Now check your answers.

▶ **Exercise 4 (Recordings 13.1, 13.2, 13.3, 13.4, 13.5)** Pronunciation practice. Listen and repeat the words on the recording. Use the transcript at the back of the book to help you if necessary.

In use

Reading

Before you start, check you know these words:

singer   concert   recording   chat   news   untidy   dirty   clean

Note: *Soap operas* are a type of television [programme/ program]. They are usually about families.

You are going to read a magazine article about celebrities and their homes.

Reading 1 Read the article – which room is Simon talking about?

My room for life

Simon Saintly, singer

People never believe me when I say that this is my [favourite/ favorite] room, but it truly is. It's a really warm room and I can just spend hours in here. It's a great place to relax after all the stress of a concert or making a new recording.

I often have friends in here too – everyone can sit round the large table and chat about their day. I really like the chairs – I bought them from a market. They're very comfortable although they don't look it. I spend so much time in here, I'm afraid I also have an old TV in the corner – I pretend to watch the news but really it's for the soap operas – and a modern hi-fi, which I play a lot of music on but never my music. I can't listen to my music.

I'm quite untidy too, as you can see. You'll always find a dirty towel or something. I really should get a cleaner. But the [cooker/stove] is always clean, I'm very careful about that, although the sink is always full. I'm like everyone, I hate doing the dishes. I should get a dishwasher but I never have the time to go shopping! Even my freezer is nearly empty, so I'll have to eat out tonight!

Reading 2 Now read the article again and find the noun that goes with the adjectives below. Be careful, one adjective is *not* used!

comfortable *chairs*   empty _____   old _____

clean _____   full _____   small _____

dirty _____   large _____   warm _____

modern _____

▶ Listening

Before you start, check you know this word:

> socket (for electricity)

Listen to Jenny and Pete as they try to arrange their bedroom.

Listening 1 (Recording 13.6) Put a ✔ next to any items of furniture that Pete or Jenny say.

✔ bed		☐ cupboard
☐ bedside cabinet		☐ quilt
☐ carpet		☐ table
☐ chair		☐ TV
☐ chest of drawers		☐ wardrobe

Listening 2 Listen to the recording again and complete the diagram of Jenny and Pete's bedroom below with the correct furniture.

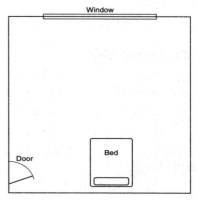

Now check your answers.

Recap

Here are the words we learned in this unit. Do you know them all? Write down the translations if necessary.

Furniture and furnishings

In the living room

table	chair	sofa
armchair	carpet	[curtains/drapes]
light	lamp	TV
[video/VCR]	hi-fi	fire
picture	plant	vase

In the kitchen

cupboard	sink	fridge
freezer	[cooker/stove]	washing machine
dishwasher	plate	bowl
cup	glass	knife
fork	spoon	

In the bathroom

bath	shower	[basin/sink]
towel	toilet	

In the bedroom

[wardrobe/closet]	chest of drawers	bedside cabinet (table)
bed	mirror	sheet
pillow	blanket	quilt

Adjectives and prepositions

(un)comfortable	heavy	light
next to	between	(on the) left/right
behind	in front of	under
on (top of)	opposite	near

Verbs and questions

There is/There are… (Is there/Are there…?)
What's in your…?
Where's your…?
What's your… like?

What to do next

- Try to describe a room in your house in detail.
- Ask someone else to describe a room in their house in English.
- Look through books or magazines to find descriptions of rooms; how much do you understand?

Why not try these units next?

- Food (1) and (2) • Shopping

Answer key for this unit

Test your basics

1 bed

2 cupboard

3 armchair

4 [curtains/drapes]

5 chest of drawers

6 lamp

7 light

8 chair

9 sofa

11 table

10 [wardrobe/closet]

12 carpet

Exercise 1

S	G	U	T	O	W	E	L	X	U	E	L	V	N
P	D	I	T	W	N	L	P	H	I	F	E	V	B
O	A	S	D	U	N	D	L	M	R	S	O	F	A
O	J	T	M	E	B	O	W	L	O	C	T	S	D
N	N	T	E	J	O	W	V	B	I	S	R	T	D
Y	P	E	P	P	I	L	L	O	W	B	E	O	I
W	V	L	S	A	G	S	K	L	I	N	E	I	P
S	R	E	D	F	R	E	E	Z	E	R	R	L	N
S	O	V	Z	N	E	J	O	P	C	S	N	E	W
H	L	I	O	U	S	B	R	I	B	N	A	T	D
E	B	S	H	O	W	E	R	L	E	C	O	G	T
E	F	I	C	J	E	C	N	Q	D	T	I	H	S
T	O	O	B	I	A	R	M	C	H	A	I	R	E
H	R	N	M	D	Q	V	P	R	I	A	V	S	L

bathroom	bedroom	living room	kitchen
shower	bed	armchair	spoon
toilet	sheet	sofa	bowl
towel	pillow	television	freezer

Exercise 2

1 The [video/VCR] is under *the TV*.
2 The plates are in *the kitchen cupboard*.
3 The bed is between *the wardrobe and the window*.
4 The towel is next to *the [basin/sink]*.
5 The [curtain/drape] is in front of *the window*.
6 The quilt is on *the bed*.
7 The freezer is on the left of *the fridge*.
8 The picture is on *the wall*.
9 There's a plant on *the table*.
(*the vase* is not used.)

Exercise 3

1 Where's the hi-fi?

   c It's on the chest of drawers, behind the sofa.

2 Have you got a television?

   b Yes, we have. And we've got a [video/VCR] too.

3 What's in this cupboard?

   d Oh, just some plates, bowls, knives, forks, and spoons.

4 Is there a table in your living room?

   No answer for this question.

5 What's your living room like?

   a It's quite big. We've got two armchairs and a great big comfortable sofa to sit on.

Reading

Reading 1 Kitchen

Reading 2

comfortable *chairs*   empty *freezer*   old *TV*
clean *[cooker/stove]*   full *sink*   ~~small~~
dirty *towel*   large *table*   warm *room*
                  modern *hi-fi*

Listening

Listening 1

- ✔ bed
- ✔ bedside cabinet
- ✘ carpet
- ✔ chair
- ✔ chest of drawers

- ✘ cupboard
- ✘ quilt
- ✔ table
- ✔ TV
- ✔ wardrobe

Listening 2

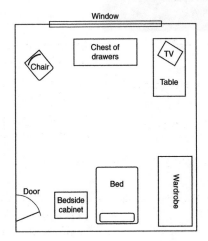

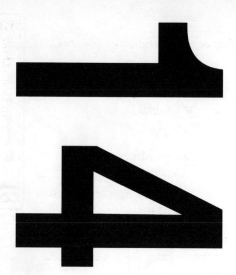

14

people and jobs

In this unit you will learn
- the names of many jobs
- words for place of
  work/conditions at work
  (office, friendly…)
- how to ask questions
  about/describe your job

Basics

Do you know these words? Check in a dictionary and write the word in your language.

1 police officer (policeman or policewoman)

_____

2 lawyer

_____

3 doctor

_____

4 nurse

_____

5 teacher

_____

6 student

_____

7 engineer

_____

8 businesswoman or businessman

_____

9 secretary

_____

10 farmer

_____

11 housewife or househusband

_____

Test your basics

Write the English word in the space provided. Don't look at page 175!

1

student

2

_____

3

_____

4

_____

5

_____

6

_____

7

_____

8

_____

9

_____

10

_____

11

_____

Extension

People and types of work

- A **worker** is someone who works; your **manager** is someone who tells you what to do (we often use the informal word **boss**); a **colleague** is someone who works with you.

- You can work for a **company**, for example, Microsoft; some people work for the **government**; these people are called **civil servants**.

- Some jobs need a lot of **training** (verb = **train**): for example **law** (lawyer), **medicine** (doctor), or **education** (teacher); these jobs are called **professions** and the people are called **professionals**. They often have to **study** for **exams** to become **qualified** to do their job.

- A new area of work is **IT** (information technology) – this is work with computers and electronics.

Places and conditions of work

- Businessmen and women and secretaries usually work in an **office**; a **factory** is a place that makes things, for example cars; a farmer works on a **farm**; a doctor can work in a **hospital** or a [**surgery/doctor's office**] – a [**surgery/doctor's office**] is smaller than a hospital; teachers work in a **school**; more and more people are now working **at home**.

- Most people work to **earn** money (**get paid**); they also get some weeks of [**holiday/vacation**] when they don't have to work.

Describing jobs and colleagues

Look at these opposites:

- To give a general idea we can say a job is **wonderful** (☺) or **awful** (☹).

- An office where the people like each other is **friendly**; the opposite is **unfriendly**.

- You like to do a job which is **interesting**, but one which is **boring** will send you to sleep.

- Employers who are **generous** give a lot to their employees; the opposite of generous is **mean**.

- If managers are **strict**, then you must do what they say; the opposite is **easy-going**.

- Managers who are **polite** always says 'please' and 'thank you'; the opposite is **rude**.
- If you are **shy** at work, then you are not happy with people you don't know well; the opposite is **self-confident**.
- Someone who helps a lot is **helpful**; the opposite is **unhelpful**.
- A colleague who is **sensitive** always thinks about other people's feelings; the opposite is **insensitive**.

Questions and sentences

About work

What are your hours?	I work from... until...
Where do you work?	I work (in an office/in a factory/at home...).
What do you do? or What's your job?	I'm a...
Who do you work for?	I work for...
How much do you earn (get paid)?	I get... a week/month/year. (**Note:** it is rude to ask this question in the UK or the US.)
How much [holiday/vacation] do you get?	I get... weeks a year.
What's... like?	He's/She's...

Examples:

When do you work?	I work from 9a.m. until 5p.m.
Where do you work?	I work in a small office.
What's your job?	I'm a teacher.
Who do you work for?	I work for the government.
How much do you get paid?	I get £20,000/$35,000 a year.
How much [holiday/vacation] do you get?	I get four weeks' [holiday/vacation] a year.
What's your boss like?	She's great. She's really friendly and helpful.

Practice

Exercise 1 Can you do this crossword?

Across

1 The opposite of boring
4 How much do you get _____?
  $20,000
5 A place that makes cars
7 Another example of 4 down
8 The opposite of easy-going
9 People who work are called
  _____

Down

1 Another term for computer
  work
2 Civil servants work for the
  _____
3 You might find a secretary
  here
4 The law is an example of a
  _____
6 For difficult jobs you often
  need _____

Exercise 2 Use the box below to complete the questions or answers about Katherine Summers.

Katherine Summers

34 years old
Computer engineer for Juice Computers in the United States
Place of work: factory in California
Hours: 8a.m. – 6p.m.
Pay: $50,000
[Holiday/Vacation]: 4 weeks a year
Colleagues: friendly, and easy-going

For example:

What's your name?   Katherine Summers

How old are you?   _I'm 34 years old_

1 _____?   I work for Juice Computers.
2 Where do you work?   _____
3 What do you do?   _____
4 _____?   I work from 8 a.m. until 6 p.m.
5 How much [holiday/
vacation] do you get a year?   _____
6 _____?   I get $50,000 a year.
7 _____?   Really friendly and easy-going.

Exercise 3 Fill the gaps with the correct word from the box on page 181. Be careful – one of the words is not used.

1 Mr Stevens asked his ___secretary___ to write a letter to the bank.
2 I work with a _____ in a small office in London.
3 George was very _____ when I first joined the company and helped me a lot.
4 To become a lawyer you have to pass lots of _____ before you become _____.
5 I don't think Jane likes me, she's always so _____.
6 How much do you get paid? £15,000? Your company is so _____!

7 'Richard! The _____ wants to see you right now.' 'OK, I'm coming.'
8 He always says 'please' and 'thank you'. It's nice to work for someone who's so _____ for a change.

| boss | businesswoman | colleague | exams | friendly |
| mean | polite | qualified | ~~secretary~~ | unfriendly |

Now check your answers.

▶ **Exercise 4 (Recordings 14.1, 14.2, 14.3, 14.4, 14.5)** Pronunciation practice. Listen and repeat the words on the recording. Use the transcript at the back of the book to help you if necessary.

In use

Reading

Before you start, check you know these words:

| island | strangers | companions | classroom | pub |

Note: *A round of drinks* is when you buy everyone in your group a drink.

You are going to read an extract from a novel, *Everyone but the Busman*, about a group of strangers who go to live for a month on a tropical island. NOTE: A *busman's holiday* is going somewhere on [holiday/vacation] where you end up doing your normal job.

Reading 1 Put a ✔ next to the jobs that are mentioned. Be careful, one job *isn't* used.

	businessman		housewife		lawyer
	nurse		police officer		teacher

As Tom woke up the next morning, he knew there really was no turning back. This was it. He was stuck here, on this boat, off to an unknown island with a group of strangers.

Tom decided to spend the morning studying his companions. What did he know? All right, the women first. Stella: well, he hadn't been surprised to hear she was a police officer. With her strict manner, she was made for the job. Just the opposite of shy Liz, the housewife. And then there was Fiona... She'd been so rude and unfriendly, Tom couldn't believe she worked as a nurse!

As for the men, well, Eric seemed friendly and easy-going. He had told them he was a teacher and Tom could imagine why he had wanted to leave the classroom. Finally, of course, there was Frank. Unbelievably mean, Frank was the only one who had not bought a round of drinks at the pub. Little surprise that he was a businessman and, Tom thought, probably a very good one.

Reading 2 Look back at the text above and fill in the missing information below. Do not write anything in the 'Listening' column yet.

Name	Job	Character	Listening
Stella	*police officer*	*strict*	
Liz			
Fiona			
Eric			
Frank			

▶ Listening

Before you start, check you know this word:

> useful

Everyone but the Busman was also turned into a radio play but was changed slightly. You are going to listen to a part of the play.

Listening 1 (Recording 14.6) Listen and write down the name of the missing character (Stella, Liz, Fiona, Eric or Frank).

Listening 2 Look back at the table for **Reading 2**. Listen again and write down any details that are different in the radio play in the 'listening' column.

Now check your answers.

Recap

Here are the words we learned in this unit. Do you know them all? Write down the translations if you need to.

People

police officer	lawyer	doctor
(policeman *or*	teacher	student
policewoman)	businessman	secretary
nurse	*or* businesswoman	farmer
engineer	worker	colleague
civil servant	manager	boss
housewife *or*		
househusband		

Types of work

company	government	profession
law	education	(professional)
IT	study	medicine
training	qualified	

Places and conditions

office	factory	farm
hospital	[surgery/	school
at home	doctor's office]	get paid
[holiday/vacation]	earn	

Jobs and colleagues

wonderful	awful	(un)friendly
interesting	boring	generous
mean	strict	easy-going
polite	rude	shy
self-confident	(un)helpful	(in)sensitive

What to do next

- Look up the names of other jobs in English.
- Try to describe a friend or a family member and what he/she does.
- Write a letter to a real or imaginary friend; write about your new job and your new colleagues. Ask questions about his/her job.

Why not try this unit next?

- Time (1)

Answer key for this unit

Test your basics

1   student

2   teacher

3   businesswoman

4   nurse

5   police officer

6   doctor

7   househusband

8   farmer

9 lawyer   10 engineer

11 secretary

Exercise 1

		¹I	n	t	e	r	e	s	t	i	n	²g	
		T										o	
						³o						v	
	⁴p	a	i	d		f						e	
	r				⁵f	a	c	⁶t	o	r	y	
	o				i			r		n		
	f				c			a		m		
⁷m	e	d	i	c	i	n	e			i	n	e
	s							n		n		
	s					⁸s	t	r	i	c	t	
	i							i		n		
⁹w	o	r	k	e	r	s		n		g		
	n											

Exercise 2

1 *Who do you work for?*	I work for Juice Computers.
2 Where do you work?	*I work in a factory in California.*
3 What do you do?	*I'm a computer engineer.*
4 *When do you work?*	I work from 8a.m. until 6p.m.
5 How much [holiday/ vacation] do you get a year?	*I get 4 weeks' [holiday/ vacation] a year.*
6 *How much do you get paid/ earn?*	I get $50,000 a year.
7 *What are your colleagues like?*	Really friendly and easy-going.

Note: Watch your grammar on question 7 – colleagues is plural!

Exercise 3

1 Mr Stevens asked his *secretary* to write a letter to the bank.
2 I work with a *colleague* in a small office in London.
3 George was very *friendly* when I first joined the company and helped me a lot.
4 To become a lawyer you have to pass lots of *exams* before you become *qualified*.
5 I don't think Jane likes me, she's always so *unfriendly*.
6 How much do you get paid? £15,000? Your company is so *mean*!
7 'Richard! The *boss* wants to see you right now.' 'OK, I'm coming.'
8 He always says 'please' and 'thank you'. It's nice to work for someone who's so *polite* for a change.

Reading

Reading 1

(*businesswoman* is not used)

✔	businessman	✔	housewife	✘	~~lawyer~~
✔	nurse	✔	police officer	✔	teacher

Reading 2

Name	Job	Character	Listening
Stella	police officer	strict	
Liz	housewife	shy	
Fiona	nurse	unfriendly, rude	
Eric	teacher	friendly, easy-going	
Frank	businessman	mean	

Listening

Listening 1

Frank is the missing character.

Name	Job	Character	Listening
Stella	~~police officer~~	strict	businesswoman
Liz	housewife	~~shy~~	self-confident
Fiona	nurse	~~unfriendly, rude~~	friendly
Eric	~~teacher~~	friendly, easy-going	engineer
Frank	businessman	mean	✗

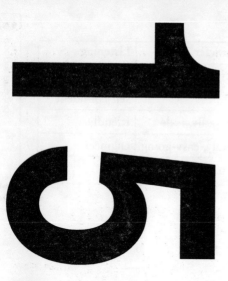

15

shopping

In this unit you will learn
- the names of many shops
- words for measures/
  numbers in a shop (pint,
  a half...)
- how to ask for what you
  want in a shop

Basics

shopping

189

15

Note: In British English, you buy something at a *shop*; in American English you buy something at a *store*.

Do you know these words? Check in a dictionary and write the word in your language.

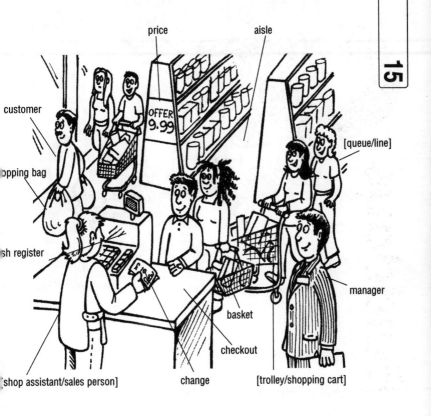

price

aisle

customer

[queue/line]

shopping bag

cash register

manager

basket

checkout

[shop assistant/sales person]

change

[trolley/shopping cart]

Test your basics

Write the English words below. Don't look at page 189!

Extension

Some common [shops/stores]

- A **bank** is somewhere you go to save or take out your money.
- A [**chemist/pharmacy**] is somewhere that sells medicines, health products and personal cleaning goods (soap, shampoo, etc.).
- In Britain, you buy newspapers from a **newsagent's** which also sells [**sweets/candy**]. In America, you buy newspapers from a **news stand** and you go to a **candy store** for [**sweets/candy**].

- An [off-licence/liquor store] sells alcoholic drinks.
- A **supermarket** sells many things, like food, soap, washing powder, etc.
- At a **post office** you can buy stamps, and often pens, envelopes, etc.
- A [**petrol station/gas station**] sells [petrol/gas] for cars, motorbikes, etc.
- A **travel agent's** is somewhere you go when you want to buy a holiday, plane tickets, etc.
- An [**estate agent's/realtor**] is somewhere that sells houses and property.

Measures and numbers

Measures

- To measure liquids, for example milk, we use [**litres/liters**]. In Britain we sometimes use **pints** for things you can drink, for example beer and milk, but [petrol/gas] is sold in [litres/liters] (1 UK pint = 0.56 [litres/liters]; 1 US pint = 0.47 [litres/liters]).
- For things we sell in weight, like meat or fruit and vegetables, we use **kilos** (kg); in Britain and America we also use **pounds** (lb) (1kg = 2.2 pounds).

Numbers

- $^1/_2$ is a **half**; $^1/_4$ is a **quarter**; $^3/_4$ is **three quarters**. We can use these with liquid or weight measures, for example:

  Half a [litre/liter] of milk.

  A quarter of a pound of butter.

- Some things are sold in **boxes**: for example, a box of [washing powder/soap powder].
- You can also buy things in **tubes**: for example, a tube of toothpaste.
- [Shops/stores] also sell products in [**packets/packages**], for example, a [packet/package] of biscuits.

Verbs

- [Shops/stores] **sell** things to their customers; customers **buy** things from a [shop/store].
- To buy something you will need to **pay** for it, that is give money for it.

- We use the verb **cost** to say how much money is needed to buy it, for example, this table costs $50.
- Past tenses: be careful, many of these verbs have irregular past tenses:

buy – **bought**   pay – **paid**
cost – **cost**   sell – **sold**

Phrases

- To ask for the times when a [shop/store] is open, we can say **What time does... open/close?**, for example:

  What time does the bank open? At ten o'clock.

- To ask about opening times: **What time do you open/close?**
- To ask for something: **I'd like...** = **I would like...** or **May I have...?**
- To ask if a [shop/store] has something: **Have you got a...?** (singular) or **Have you got any...?** (plural and uncountables) or **Do you sell...?**
- To ask for a price: **How much does... cost?** or **What's the price of...?**

You might hear a [shop assistant/sales person] use the following phrases:

- Giving opening times: **We open** *or* **close at...**
- Offering help: **Can I help you? Anything else?**
- Agreeing: **Certainly. Of course.**
- Saying no: **Sorry, no. I'm afraid not.**
- Asking about quantity: **How much/many would you like?**

Examples:

Can I help you?
Certainly. How much would you like?
Anything else?
I'd like a [packet/package] of cigarettes, please.
And can I have a box of matches?
How much does this cost?
Do you sell newspapers?
What time do you close?

Yes, have you got any milk?
Half a [litre/liter], please.

No, that's all, thanks.
Of course.

I'm sorry, I'm afraid we don't have any.
Twenty pounds.
Sorry, no.
At six o'clock.

Practice

Exercise 1 Can you do this crossword?

Down

1 (And **2 across**) We come here to buy stamps
3 'How much does this _____?'
4 In British English we say 'shop', in American English we say _____
5 In American English we say 'news stand', in British English we say _____
6 A _____, a half, three quarters...
8 The person who runs a shop is the _____
11 A _____ is about 2 pounds

Across

2 (See **1 down**)
7 A _____ buys things in a [shop/store]
9 A _____ is about half a [litre/liter]
10 You carry things in a [shop/store] in a _____
12 [Shops/stores] _____ things to you

Exercise 2 Match a word on the left with one on the right.

1 A tube of ————————— milk

2 A [packet/package] of   cheese

3 Half   [sweets/candy]

4 A pound of   toothpaste

5 Three quarters   [washing power/soap powder]

6 A box of   a [litre/liter]

7 A [litre/liter] of   of a kilo

Exercise 3 Put the conversation between a shop assistant and a customer below into the correct order.

a Certainly, sir. How much would you like? *3*
b Two [litres/liters].
c £7.63 please, sir.
d Can I help you? *1*
e I'm sorry, I'm afraid we don't.
f Here you are.
g Thank you, goodbye.
h Yes, I'd like some milk, please. *2*
i Of course, sir. How much cheese would you like?
j Thank you, sir. Here's your change.
k Goodbye.
l Half a pound, please. Do you sell newspapers?
m Oh well, never mind. How much is that?
n Right then, two [litres/liters]. Anything else?
o Yes, have you got any cheese?

Now check your answers.

▶ **Exercise 4 (Recordings 15.1, 15.2, 15.3, 15.4, 15.5)** Pronunciation practice. Listen and repeat the words on the recording. Use the transcript at the back of the book to help you if you need to.

In use

Reading

Before you start, check you know these words:

| internet website maintain deliver (noun: delivery) |
| Ferrari free |

Note: *To register* is to put your name and details down for something, for example a language course.

Many people now shop using the internet. This is called on-line shopping. You're going to read a website from an American on-line store.

Reading 1 Look at the list of advantages of on-line shopping. Put a ✔ next to the ones in the text.

Free delivery	☐	Low prices	☐
Good choice	☐	No queues	☐

Welcome to www.buyithere.com,
the web shopping experience!

Are you...
   tired of high prices?
   tired of long queues?
   tired of poor choice?

Then this is the website for you! www.buyithere.com is the shopping experience that takes the hassle out and puts the fun back into shopping. We have...

✓ **Low prices:** With no stores to maintain and no sales people to pay, all our money goes into making our prices as low as they can possibly be! Like a box of Zip! washing powder, only $2.50.

✓ **No lines:** Wait no longer than the time it takes you to click your mouse. With www.buyithere.com, you can do all your shopping in little more than five minutes! And we're open 24 hours a day, seven days a week, so you'll never find us closed.

✓ **Great choice:** We shop around the world bringing you anything you could possibly think of, from a pound of cheese to a Ferrari, all delivered straight to your door.

Tired of ordinary stores? Try us. First take five minutes to register (it's free) and then you're away. Click here to enter!

Enter

Reading 2 Now answer the following questions.

1 What is the name of the company? *The company's name is www.buyithere.com*
2 How many stores does it have?
3 How much is a box of Zip! washing powder
4 When is it open?
5 What can you buy?
6 How much does it cost to register?

▶ Listening

Before you start, check you know these words:

beef	wine	strawberries	peaches	deliver

The supermarket Coset has started doing telephone sales.

Listening 1 Look at the food and drinks below. Listen to the telephone conversation and put a ✔ next to the foods Mrs. Jones buys.

beef		beer		bread
peaches		strawberries		wine

Listening 2 Listen again and match the two parts of the questions below. Be careful, one of the questions is *not* heard.

1 Can I have...   a any strawberries?
2 Do you have...   b is that?
3 How many...   c three pounds of minced beef?
4 How much...   d would you like?
5 Would you like...   e some peaches?
6 When will...   f it be delivered?

Now check your answers.

Recap

Here are the words we learned in this unit. Do you know them all? Write down the translations if you need to.

In a [shop/store]

[shop assistant/ sales person]	[trolley/ shopping cart]	customer
basket	shopping bag	manager
cash register	checkout	price
aisle		[queue/line]

Common [shops/stores]

bank	[chemist/pharmacy]
[newsagent's/news stand]	[off-licence/liquor store]
supermarket	post office
travel agent's	[estate agent's/realtor]
[petrol station/gas station]	

Measures and numbers

[litre/liter]	pint	kilo
pound	a quarter	a half
three-quarters	box	tube
[packet/package]		

Verbs

sell (sold)	buy (bought)	pay (paid)
cost (cost)		

Phrases

What time do you/ does... open/close?	I'd like...	Can I have...?
Have you got...?	Do you sell...?	How much does... cost?
Can I help you?	Anything else?	Certainly.
Of course	Sorry, no.	I'm afraid not.
How much/many would you like?		

What to do next

- If you can, try shopping in an English-speaking [shop/store]. If not, imagine yourself in an English-speaking [shop/store] – what do you say?
- If you have access to the internet, look for an on-line store in English.

Why not try these units next?

- Clothes (1) • Food (1)

Answer key for this unit

Test your basics

Check your answers on page 189 (Basics).

Exercise 1

Exercise 2

1 A tube of *toothpaste*
2 A [packet/package] of *[sweets/candy]*
3 Half a *[litre/liter]*

4 A pound of *cheese*
5 Three quarters *of a kilo*
6 A box of [*washing powder/soap powder*]
7 A [litre/liter] of *milk*

Exercise 3

d Can I help you?
h Yes, I'd like some milk, please.
a Certainly, sir. How much would you like?
b Two litres.
n Right then, two litres. Anything else?
o Yes, have you got any cheese?
i Of course, sir. How much cheese would you like?
l Half a pound, please. Do you sell newspapers?
e I'm sorry, I'm afraid we don't.
m Oh well, never mind. How much is that?
c £7.63 please, sir.
f Here you are.
j Thank you, sir. Here's your change.
g Thank you, goodbye.
k Goodbye.

Reading

Reading 1

~~Free delivery~~ ☒   Low prices

Good choice   No queues ✔

Reading 2

1 The company's name is www.buyithere.com
2 It has no stores (it's a website).
3 A box of Zip! washing powder costs $2.50.
4 It's open 24 hours a day, seven days a week.
5 You can buy anything you want (for example a pound of cheese or a Ferrari).
6 It costs nothing to register (it's free).

Listening

Listening 1

beef	✔	beer	✗	bread	✔
peaches	✔	strawberries	✗	wine	✔

(**Note:** They don't have any strawberries.)

Listening 1

1 Can I have…
2 Do you have…
3 How many…
4 How much…
5 Would you like…
6 When will…

c three pounds of minced beef?
a any strawberries?
d would you like?
b is that?
e some peaches? (*not used*)
f it be delivered?

time (1)

In this unit you will learn
- the names of the days/months/seasons (Monday, January, Spring…)
- dates and years (twenty-third [23rd], two thousand and three [2003])
- how to ask about days/dates (What day is it? When's your birthday?)

Basics

Do you know these words? Check in a dictionary and write the word in your language.

1 day
_____

A day has 24 hours.

2 week
_____

A week has seven days.

3 month
_____

A month normally has 30 or 31 days.

4 year
_____

A year normally has 365 days.

5 leap year
_____

A leap year has 366 days and comes every four years.

6 date
_____

The date is the day, month and year, for example: 24/4/02 (UK) or 4/24/02 (US).

7 calendar
_____

A calendar is a table of all the dates in a year.

8 diary
_____

A diary is a notebook which shows every day in the year. You can use it to write down dates you need to remember, your future plans, or what you have done.

Test Your Basics

Cover page 202 so you can't see the words. Then fill in the spaces below.

16

1 This normally has 30 or 31 days. _month_

2 This has 24 hours. _____

3 For example, 15/5/05 or 5/15/05. _____

4 This normally has 365 days... _____

5 ...but this one has 366 days! _____

6 A notebook to write appointments or what you did. _____

7 A table with all the (no. 3) in a (no. 4). _____

8 This has seven days. _____

Extension

Days and months

- Here are the seven days of the week in order:
  Monday, Tuesday, Wednesday, Thursday, Friday, Saturday, Sunday.
- Monday to Friday are all **week days**; Saturday and Sunday are the **weekend**.
- Here are the twelve months of the year in order:
  January, February, March, April, May, June, July, August, September, October, November, December.

Dates and years

- For years up to 1999 we normally say, for example, nineteen ninety-nine (1999); for '00' years we say 'hundred'. For example, 1900 = nineteen hundred.

- For 2000 upwards we say two thousand, two thousand and one, two thousand and two...

- Look at this date: [23 June/June 23].
  Be careful how you say the number: we don't say twenty-three, we say **twenty-third**. Look at the box below to help you with these numbers – the difficult ones are in **bold**.

1st	**first**	11th	eleventh	21st	twenty-first
2nd	**second**	12th	**twelfth**	22nd	twenty-second
3rd	**third**	13th	thirteenth	23rd	twenty-third
4th	fourth	14th	fourteenth	24th	twenty-fourth
5th	**fifth**	15th	fifteenth	25th	twenty-fifth
6th	sixth	16th	sixteenth	26th	twenty-sixth
7th	seventh	17th	seventeenth	27th	twenty-seventh
8th	eighth	18th	eighteenth	28th	twenty-eighth
9th	**ninth**	19th	nineteenth	29th	twenty-ninth
10th	tenth	20th	**twentieth**	30th	**thirtieth**
				31st	thirty-first

Note: We can write and say dates in two ways. We write **23rd June** or **June 23rd** or just [**23 June/June 23**]. We say 'the twenty-third of June' or 'June the twenty-third'.

Seasons and special dates

- Most countries have four **seasons**. In the northern hemisphere, when it's very cold, it's **winter**; next is **spring**; next, when it's hot, it's **summer**; then last it's [**autumn/fall**].

  Countries in the north and south have seasons at opposite times; look at the months and the seasons in Britain.

Winter	December – February	**Spring**	March to May
Summer	June – August	**Autumn**	September – November

- There are also special days or **holidays** in the calendar: for example, in Britain and America, **Christmas** is in December; **Christmas Day** is on December 25th and **Easter** is in March or April.

- Days like Christmas Day are **public holidays**; in Britain they are called **bank holidays**.
- People also have special days: for example, your **birthday** (the day you were born).

  When's your birthday?   November 16th.

Prepositions

Be careful to use the correct preposition with time expressions:

- **On** + days and dates; **in** + month/year/seasons/'the week'; **at** + holidays (e.g. Easter).

  Note: British English uses **at** + 'the weekend' but American English uses **on** + 'the weekend'.

  Examples:
  At Christmas (period), but *on* Christmas Day (because it's a day).
  In May (month), but *on* May 5th (because it's a date).
  In the week but [*at/on*] weekends.

Questions

- To find out the day/month/year/date we ask **What...is it?**

  What day/month/year/date   It's Monday/September/
     is it?   2002/January 17th.

- To know when something happens, for example, a birthday or Easter, we ask **When's...?**

  When's your birthday?   It's on [1 September/
                            September 1].
  When's Easter?   This year it's on [24th
                            March/March 24th].

Practice

Exercise 1 Make the correct word from the anagrams below, then put the words in the correct list, in order. There are four days, five months and three seasons.

1	o y d a m n	*Monday*	7	t s u u g a
2	r e w n i t	*winter*	8	n u t a m u
3	d s n u a y		9	g i n r p s
4	l i p a r		10	r e n v o m e b
5	m e m s u r		11	y i d r a f
6	y d a h u r s t		12	y a n j u r a

Days	Months	Seasons
Monday		*winter*

Exercise 2 Fill the gaps with the correct preposition *on*, *in* or *at*.

1 I'll see you _on_ Monday.
2 ____ the week I normally get home at six o'clock.
3 My wife always brings me breakfast in bed ____ my birthday.
4 We're going to Spain ____ March.
5 Ben woke up at four o'clock ____ Christmas Day.
6 Are you doing anything ____ the weekend?
7 We were married ____ 1992.
8 The roads are always very busy ____ Christmas.
9 We're having a party ____ January 5th.

Exercise 3 Look at the following sentences and decide if they are right (✔) or wrong (✗), then correct those that are wrong.

1 Why don't you come around on Saterday? ✗ Why don't you come around on **Saturday**?
2 'What day is it?' 'It's Friday.' ✔
3 Our daughter was born in the year twenty hundred.
4 'When's your birthday?' 'On 6th April.'
5 I'm seeing the doctor on Wendsday.
6 'Are you free on Tuesday?' 'I'll look in my calendar and check.'
7 We always visit our grandparents at Easter.
8 This winter was really cold.

9 'What date is your birthday this year?' 'It's on Sunday.'
10 I hate February. It's a horrible month.

Now check your answers.

▶ **Exercise 4 (Recordings 16.1, 16.2, 16.3, 16.4, 16.5)** Pronunciation practice. Listen and repeat the words on the recording. Use the transcript at the back of the book to help you if necessary.

In use

Reading

Do you know these words?

| president | elect | leader | independent | racism |
| shoot (shot) | prison | release | musicians |

Notes: In Britain all dates written in numbers are day/month/year – for example, 2/3/1999 is 2 March 1999 (not 3 February). In America, all dates written in numbers are month/day/year, so 2/3/1999 is February 3 1999 (not March 2). The *White House* is the home of the president of the United States. The *Beatles* were a rock band from Liverpool who were extremely successful. To *split up* is when a group of people leave each other.

An *encyclopedia* is a book that gives us information about many things. What do you know about these people – Bill Clinton, Gandhi, Nelson Mandela, Paul McCartney and Eva Peron? You are now going to read five short pieces about these people taken from a British encyclopedia.

Reading 1 Underline each date reference below (you should find thirteen).

Bill Clinton

Bill Clinton, born 19/8/1946 was elected president in November 1992, and left the White House in 2001. A Democrat, he proved a very popular president, even though he had one or two personal and political troubles while in the White House.

Mohandas Karamchand Gandhi

This great political leader who helped India become independent was born on 2/10/1869. He led a long fight against racism, but was never violent. He was shot and killed on 30/1/1948. He was born into a family...

Nelson Mandela

A popular hero, Nelson Mandela was born on 18/7/1918 and would spend many years in prison, before his release on 2/11/1991. He became the first black president of South Africa in 1994. His early life...

Paul McCartney

Born on 18/6/1942, Paul McCartney is one of the most famous pop musicians ever and was a member of the greatest rock-and-roll band of all time, the Beatles. After the Beatles split up in 1970, he had more success with Wings, who...

Eva Peron

Known to many in her native country of Argentina as 'Evita', Eva Peron was born on 7/5/1919 and died young on 26/7/1952. She married General Peron in 1945 and, after he became president, quickly became extremely popular herself. Evita, though, was...

Reading 2 Look at these sentences and decide if they are right (✔) or wrong (✗). Then correct those that are wrong.

1 Bill Clinton was elected President in November 1992. ✔
2 Gandhi was born on February 10, 1869. ✗ Gandhi was born on **October 2,** 1869.
3 Eva Peron married in 1952.
4 Paul McCartney was born in June 1942.
5 Nelson Mandela left prison on 11th February 1991.
6 Eva Peron's birthday was 7 May.
7 The Beatles split up in 1970.
8 Gandhi was killed in March 1948.
9 Nelson Mandela became president in 1994.
10 Bill Clinton was born on 1946.

▶ Listening

Before you start, check you know these words:

> celebrity (person)   actor/actress   tragically   hospital
> star (verb)   release (of a film)

Note: A *car crash* is a very bad accident in a car. A *smash hit* is an informal word to describe a very successful [film/movie] – for example, *Titanic* was a smash hit.

Times Of My Life is a radio show where celebrities talk about their lives. You're going to hear the introduction to one show where some information is given about that week's celebrity.

Listening 1 (Recording 16.6) Listen to the recording and number the dates that you hear in the order you hear them. Be careful, two of the dates are not on the recording. Do not do anything with the listening 2 column yet.

Dates		**Listening 2**
October 1958	☐	She was born.
May 4th 1962	☑	She was married.
1986	☐	She had a son.
1988	☐	She had a serious car crash.
1990	☐	Her father died.
Christmas Day 1992	☐	She made her first [film/movie].
March 1997	☐	She starred in *Conflict of the*
Last year	☐	*Galaxies.*
1st January 2000	☐	*Conflict of the Galaxies II* released.
Next month	☐	

Listening 2 Now match the date with what happened in the second column.

Now check your answers.

Recap

Here are the words we learned in this unit. Do you know them all? Write down the translations if necessary.

Nouns

day	week	weekdays
weekend	month	year
leap year	date	calendar
diary		

Days

Monday	Tuesday	Wednesday
Thursday	Friday	Saturday
Sunday		

Months

January	February	March
April	May	June
July	August	September
October	November	December

Dates and years

first, second, third, fourth...	1900, 1999, 2000, 2011...	1st January, 2nd February, March 12th, May 20th...

Seasons and special dates

winter	spring	summer
[autumn/fall]	Christmas	Christmas Day
Easter	public holiday	bank holiday
birthday		

Prepositions

on	in	at

Questions

What...is it?	When's...?

What to do next

- Make a list of important dates for you (for example, birthdays, holidays…) and see if you can say them in English.
- Find any dates you can in English books, magazines and newspapers – can you say them in English?

Why not try this unit next?

- Time (2)

Answer key for this unit

Test your basics

1	This normally has 30 or 31 days	month
2	This has 24 hours	day
3	For example, 15/5/05 or 5/15/05	date
4	This normally has 365 days…	year
5	…but this one has 366 days!	leap year
6	A notebook to write appointments or what you did	diary
7	A plan with all the (no 3.) in a (no. 4)	calendar
8	This has seven days	week

Exercise 1

1	o y d a m n	Monday	7	t s u u g a	August
2	r e w n i t	winter	8	n u t a m u	autumn
3	d s n u a y	Sunday	9	g i n r p s	spring
4	l i p a r	April	10	r e n v o m e b	November
5	m e m s u r	summer	11	y i d r a f	Friday
6	y d a h u r s t	Thursday	12	y a n j u r a	January

Days	Months	Seasons
Monday	January	winter
Thursday	April	spring
Friday	August	summer
Sunday	November	[autumn/fall]

Exercise 2

1 I'll see you *on* Monday.
2 *In* the week I normally get back at six o'clock from work.
3 My wife always brings me breakfast in bed *on* my birthday.
4 We're going to Spain *in* March.
5 Ben woke up at four o'clock *on* Christmas Day.
6 Are you doing anything [*at/on*] the weekend?
7 We were married *in* 1992.
8 The roads are always very busy *at* Christmas.
9 We're having a party *on* January 5th.

Exercise 3

1 Why don't you come around on Saterday? ✗ Why don't you come around on **Saturday**?
2 'What day is it?' 'It's Friday.' ✔
3 Our daughter was born in the year twenty hundred. ✗ Our daughter was born in the year **two thousand**.
4 'When's your birthday?' 'On 6th April.' ✔
5 I'm seeing the doctor on Wendsday. ✗ I'm seeing the doctor on **Wednesday**.
6 'Are you free on Tuesday?' 'I'll look in my calendar and check.' ✗ 'Are you free on Tuesday?' 'I'll look in my **diary** and check.'
7 We always visit our grandparents at Easter. ✔
8 This winter was really cold. ✔
9 'What date is your birthday this year?' 'It's on Sunday.' ✗ 'What **day** is your birthday this year?' 'It's on Sunday.'
10 I hate February. It's a horrible month. ✔

Reading

Reading 1

Bill Clinton

Bill Clinton, born *19/8/1946* was elected President in *November 1992*, and left the White House in *2001*. A Democrat, he proved a very popular president, even though he had one or two personal and political troubles while in the White House.

Mohandas Karamchand Gandhi

This great political leader who helped India become independent was born on *2/10/1869*. He led a long fight against racism, but was never violent. He was shot and killed on *30/1/1948*. He was born into a family…

Nelson Mandela

A popular hero, Nelson Mandela was born on _18/7/1918_ and would spend many years in prison, before his release on _2/11/1991_. He became the first black president of South Africa in _1994_. His early life…

Paul McCartney

Born on _18/6/1942_, Paul McCartney is one of the most famous pop musicians ever and was a member of the greatest rock and roll band of all time, the Beatles. After the Beatles split up in _1970_, he had more success with Wings, who…

Eva Peron

Known to many in her native country of Argentina as '_Evita_', Eva Peron was born on _7/5/1919_ and died young on _26/7/1952_. She married General Peron in _1945_ and after he became president quickly became extremely popular herself. Evita, though, was…

Reading 2

1 Bill Clinton was elected President in November 1993. ✔
2 Gandhi was born on February 10, 1869 ✗ Gandhi was born on **October 2** 1869.
3 Eva Peron married in 1952. ✗ Eva Peron **died** in 1952; she was married in **1945**.
4 Paul McCartney was born in June 1942. ✔
5 Nelson Mandela left prison on 11th February 1991. ✔
6 Eva Peron's birthday was 7th May. ✔
7 The Beatles split up in 1970. ✔
8 Gandhi was killed in March 1948. ✗ Gandhi was killed in **January** 1948.
9 Nelson Mandela became president in 1994. ✔
10 Bill Clinton was born on 1946. ✗ Bill Clinton was born **in** 1946.

Listening

Listening 1 and 2

Dates		Listening 2
~~October 1958~~	☒	
May 4th 1962	1	She was born.
1986	5	Her father died.
1988	2	She was married.
1990	4	She made her first [film/movie].
Christmas Day 1992	3	She had a son.
March 1997	6	She had a serious car crash.
Last year	7	She starred in *Conflict of the Galaxies*.
~~January 1st 2000~~	☒	
Next month	8	*Conflict of the Galaxies II* released.

17

time (2)

In this unit you will learn
- how to tell the time
- common verbs and words to use with time (take, early…)
- how to ask about time (What time is it? When do you…?)

Basics

Note: Before you do this unit, make sure you know the numbers 1–60 and the words from Unit 17: Time (1).

Do you know these words? Check in a dictionary and write the word in your language.

1 hour
_____

There are 24 hours in one day.

2 minute
_____

There are 60 minutes in one hour.

3 second
_____

There are 60 seconds in one minute.

4 clock
_____

5 watch
_____

6 time
_____

The hours, minutes and, sometimes, seconds together, for example twelve thirty-eight:

12:38

Test your basics

Cover the words on page 216 so you can't see them. Then write the English word in the spaces below.

Look at this number:

> 6:32:45 p.m.

1   6:32:45 p.m. is the...   *time*

2   45 is the number of...   _____

3   32 is the number of...   _____

4   6 is the number of...   _____

5   _____

6   _____

Extension

Time

- **O'clock** is on the hour, for example, 2:00 = two o'clock.

- At other times we normally use groups of five: **five, ten, twenty, twenty-five.**

- For 15 and 45 minutes we use **a quarter**; for 30 minutes we use **half.**

- We use **past** for after the hour up to 30 minutes.

  Example: 2:05 **five past two**   2:20 **twenty past two**
             2:15 **a quarter past two** 2:30 **half past two**

- After 30 minutes or **half past** the hour, we say the number of minutes **to** the next hour.

  Example 2:35 **twenty-five to three** 2:45 **a quarter to three**
          2:40 **twenty to three**   2:55 **five to three**

- We can also say the time by saying the hour and the minutes.

  Example 2:05 **two oh five**   2:35 **two thirty-five**
          2:15 **two fifteen**   2:40 **two forty**
          2:20 **two twenty**   2:45 **two forty-five**
          2:30 **two thirty**   2:55 **two fifty-five**

- The first part of the day is called **morning**. To show times in the morning we can use **a.m.**, for example: 8:15 a.m. = a quarter past eight in the morning.

- 12 p.m. is **noon**; after noon we have **afternoon**. When it gets dark, we have **evening** and at **night** people go to sleep.

  Note: be careful with prepositions; we say **in** the morning/afternoon/evening but **at** noon or **at** night.

- Here are some common verbs we use with times. Look up any you don't know:

get up	go to work/school	have dinner
	go home	go to bed

- We use the preposition **at** with times to answer the question **when?** For example:

      I get up at 6 o'clock.
      I go to bed at half past ten.

More days

- **Today** is the day now. If today is [14 September/September 14], then [13 September/September 13] was **yesterday** and [15 September/September 15] is **tomorrow**. [12 September/September 12] was **the day before yesterday** and [16 September/September 16] is **the day after tomorrow**.

- For years, months, weeks, or special occasions we can use **last** to mean the one before and **next** to mean the one after.

  Examples: Next week we're going on [holiday/vacation].
  Last month we bought a car.
  Next January I'll be sixty.
  Let's come back next year.
  We had a great time last Christmas.

- For two or more days, weeks, months, etc. we can use **ago** for the past and **in...time** for the future:

  In two weeks' time we're going on [holiday/vacation].
  Three months ago we bought a car.
  In three years' time I'll be sixty.
  We saw him three days ago.

Modifiers, nouns and verbs

- Look at these nouns which we often use with times; look up any you don't know.

meeting	holiday	wait	journey

- If you have a meeting at 9:00 and you are there at 9:00 you are **on time**; if you are there at 8:45, you are **early**, but if you're there at 9:15, then you are **late**.

- To say how long something is we can use the verb **take** (past = **took**), for example:

  The journey took three hours.

We can use the adjectives **long** and **short** to talk about how long something takes, for example: a long journey; a short wait.

Questions and sentences

- To find out the time we can ask **What time is it?** We can also ask **What time** or **When** + verb.
- For the length of time we use **How long + take + verb…?** or **How long + be + noun…?**

Examples:

What time is it?

It's half past four. *or* I don't know, I'm not wearing a watch.

What time do you have dinner?

We have dinner at seven o'clock.

How long does it take to go to work?

It takes forty minutes.

How long was your [holiday/vacation]?

It was three weeks.

Practice

Exercise 1 See if you can do this crossword.

Across

2 The day after today
3 a.m. is the…
4 (and 4 down) A quarter past five is also…
5 30 minutes = _____ an hour
7 The day before today

Down

1 The opposite of short
2 'What's the _____?' 'Ten o'clock.'
4 See 4 across
6 If you arrive before a meeting, you are…

Exercise 2 Decide if these sentences are right (✔) or wrong (✗). Then correct those that are wrong.

1 We got here the day before yesterday. ✔
2 I have an important meeting this day at ten o'clock. ✗ I have an important meeting **today** at ten o'clock.
3 I get up at thirty to eight in the morning (7:30).
4 How long time does it take you to get to work?
5 I have a short walk to work; it only takes fifteen minutes.
6 It's my birthday in two days' ago and I still don't know what to do.
7 I had a half an hour wait for the bus today.
8 We normally have dinner at seven hours.
9 The time is three forty-five; that is, it's a quarter to four.
10 At evening I like to stay in and watch TV.

Exercise 3 Put the words in the correct order to make the question, then choose the correct answer.

1 it time what is?   *What time is it?*
a About three and a half hours.
b About half past three. ✔

2 meeting is how long your?
a About fifty minutes. I'll meet you for lunch afterwards.
b About 10:50. I'll meet you for lunch afterwards.

3 get time what you do up?
a I normally get up at a quarter past seven.
b It normally takes me about twenty-five minutes.

4 time meeting what your is?
a About fifty minutes. I'll meet you for lunch afterwards.
b About 10:50. I'll meet you for lunch afterwards.

5 take to long how it does work go to?
a I normally get up at a quarter past seven.
b It normally takes me about twenty-five minutes.

Now check your answers.

▶ **Exercise 4 (Recordings 17.1, 17.2, 17.3, 17.4)** Pronunciation practice. Listen and repeat the words on the recording. Use the transcript at the back of the book to help you if necessary.

In use

Reading

Before you start, check you know these words:

> girlfriend   boyfriend   concert   tickets   argument
> train   home

The diary of Sam Jones is a novel about a young man from the countryside working in the city. Read part of Sam's diary about his relationship with Susie.

Reading 1 What is today's date, i.e. what date is the author writing now?

AUGUST 31   *New person at work today. Her name's Susie. She's really nice, I hope I get to know her better. Must ask her for a drink.*

SEPTEMBER 9   *Went to the bar, just me and Susie. Told her I really liked her; she said she liked me, too. Couldn't believe it. Asked her to be my girlfriend and she said yes! Hooray!*

SEPTEMBER 23   *It's Susie's birthday in October, and I know 'Stairway' are playing a concert on October 10. Today I bought some tickets for us both; $120 but that's love!*

SEPTEMBER 29   *Don't want to talk. Spoke to Susie. Big argument over Colin Todd. How can she do this to me?*

SEPTEMBER 30   *Not even a month and it's over! Susie phoned me at 11 and said I wasn't her boyfriend now. She is seeing Colin Todd! It's now one o'clock – I'm getting the train home. Goodbye Susie and goodbye city!*

Reading 2 Look at Sam's sentences below. Using today's date from **Reading 1** change the dates to use the vocabulary in this unit (last, next, ago, in...time, etc.).

For example: I met Susie on August 31.
                 I met Susie *last month*.

1   I asked Susie to be my girlfriend on September 9.
    I asked Susie to be my girlfriend...
2   I bought some tickets to a concert on September 23.
    I bought some tickets to a concert...

3 On September 29 I had a big argument with Susie.
...I had a big argument with Susie.
4 Susie phoned me at 11 o'clock.
Susie phoned me...
5 It's Susie's birthday in October.
It's Susie's birthday...
6 I have tickets to see *Stairway* on October 10.
I have tickets to see *Stairway*...

▶ Listening

Before you start, check you know these words:

> holiday   Greece   taxi   plane   flying   flight   hotel

Note: To offer someone a *lift* is to offer to take them somewhere in your car. We use the phrase *local time* when the time in one part of the world is different to our own; for example, Greece is two hours ahead of the UK, so if I am in Greece, and it is 10 a.m. in the UK, then it is 12 p.m. local time.

You are going to hear Bob ask Fiona about her holiday plans.

Listening 1 (Recording 17.5) Listen and put a ✔ next to the questions you hear Bob ask.

When are you going?   ☐   When are you coming back?   ☐
What time is the taxi
  coming?   ☐   How long is the flight?   ☐
What time is your flight?   ☐   When do you arrive in Greece?   ☐

Listening 2 Listen to the recording again and decide if the following sentences are right (✔) or wrong (✗), then correct those that are wrong.

1 Bob's going on holiday.   ✗   **Fiona's** going on holiday.
2 Fiona is going to Greece.   ✔
3 The taxi's coming at 6:30 p.m.
4 Last time, the plane was late.
5 She's coming back in two weeks' time.
6 The flight takes four hours.
7 After the flight, there's a long ride to the hotel.
8 They should arrive by half past four.

Now check your answers.

Recap

Here are the words we learned in this unit. Do you know them all? Write down the translations if necessary.

Time

the time	hour	minute
second	o'clock	past
to	a quarter	half
five past two	half past two	a quarter to three
(at) two twenty	a.m.	p.m.
morning	noon	afternoon
evening	night	watch
clock		

More days

today	yesterday	the day before yesterday
tomorrow	the day after tomorrow	last
next	ago	in...time

Modifiers, nouns and verbs

on time	early	late
take	long	short
meeting	[holiday/vacation]	wait

Questions

What time is it?	What time...?	How long...?
When...?		

What to do next

- What time is it now?
- Think about your day – write down what times you do things and try saying them aloud.

Why not try these units next?

• Food (1) • Weather

Answer key for this unit

Test your basics

1	6:32:45 p.m. is the...	time
2	45 is the number of...	seconds
3	32 is the number of...	minutes
4	6 is the number of...	hours
5		watch
6		clock

Exercise 1

Exercise 2

1 We got here the day before yesterday. ✔
2 I have an important meeting this day at ten o'clock. ✗ I have an important meeting **today** at ten o'clock.
3 I get up at thirty to eight in the morning. ✗ I get up at **seven thirty** in the morning or I get up at **half past seven** in the morning.
4 How long time does it take you to get to work? ✗ How long does it take you to get to work? (Don't use the word **time**).
5 I have a short walk to work; it only takes 15 minutes. ✔
6 It's my birthday in two days' ago and I still don't know what to do. ✗ It's my birthday in two days' **time** and I still don't know what to do.
7 I had a half an hour wait for the bus today. ✔
8 We normally have dinner at seven hours. ✗ We normally have dinner at **seven o'clock**.
9 The time is three forty-five, that is, it's a quarter to four. ✔
10 At evening I like to stay in and watch TV. ✗ **In the** evening I like to stay in and watch TV.

Exercise 3

1 *What time is it?*
b About half past three.

2 *How long is your meeting?*
a About fifty minutes. I'll meet you for lunch afterwards.

3 *What time do you get up?*
a I normally get up at a quarter past seven.

4 *What time is your meeting?*
b About 10:50. I'll meet you for lunch afterwards.

5 *How long does it take to go to work?*
b It normally takes me about 25 minutes.

Reading

Reading 1

Today's date is September 30.

Reading 2 Here are the suggested answers.

1 I asked Susie to be my girlfriend *three weeks ago*.
2 I bought some tickets to a concert *last week*.
3 *Yesterday* I had a big argument with Susie.

4 Susie phoned me *two hours ago.*
5 It's Susie's birthday *next month.*
6 I have tickets to see *Stairway in ten days' time.*

Listening

Listening 1

When are you going? ☑	When are you coming back? ☑
What time is the taxi coming? ☑	How long is the flight? ☑
~~What time is your flight?~~ ☒	~~When do you arrive in Greece?~~ ☒

Listening 1

1 Bob's going on holiday. ✗   **Fiona's** going on holiday.
2 Fiona is going to Greece. ✔
3 The taxi's coming at 6:30 p.m. ✗ The taxi's coming at 6:30 a.m. ('half past six in the morning')
4 Last time, the plane was late. ✗ Last time, the **taxi** was late.
5 She's coming back in two weeks' time. ✔
6 The flight takes four hours. ✔
7 After the flight, there's a long journey to the hotel. ✗ After the flight, there's a **short** journey to the hotel.
8 They should arrive by half past four. ✔

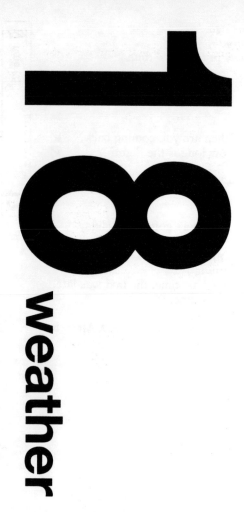

18

weather

In this unit you will learn:
- different types of weather (sunny, rain…)
- common verbs and adjectives we use for the weather (shine, wet…)
- how to ask about the weather

Basics

Do you know these words? Check in a dictionary and write the word in your language.

Nouns	Adjectives
1 sun	sunny
_____	_____
2 rain	rainy
_____	_____
3 wind	windy
_____	_____
4 cloud	cloudy
_____	_____
5 fog	foggy
_____	_____
6 snow	snowy
_____	_____
7 storm	stormy
_____	_____

Test your basics

Fill in the spaces below. Don't look at page 229!

		Noun	Adjective
1		_wind_	_windy_
2		_____	_____
3		_____	_____
4		_____	_____
5		_____	_____
6		_____	_____
7		_____	_____

Extension

Verbs and nouns

- Some kinds of weather can also be used as verbs, for example:

  I can't go out now, it's **raining**.
  In my country it always **snows** at Christmas.

- For some kinds of weather we use other verbs + noun; we use **shine** (past = **shone**) with sun and we use **blow** (past = **blew**) for wind, for example:

  Great, the sun's shining at last! Let's go out.
  The wind was really blowing hard when I walked to work today.

- During a storm you often have **thunder** (which you can hear) and **lightning** (which you can see).

- In very cold weather you will often see **frost** on the ground (adjective = **frosty**).

Adjectives and modifiers

- If it rains, then it's **wet**; the opposite is **dry**. In hot countries it's often **humid** or **sticky** just before it rains. Many tropical countries like Indonesia and Ecuador are humid.

- We can also talk about temperature:

  ❄❄ **hot**   ❄ **warm**   ❄ **cool**   ❄❄ **cold**

- In very hot weather we can say it is **boiling** and in very cold we can say it is **freezing**.

- If it is sunny, we can say it is **bright**; if it's cloudy we can call it **dull**.

- Another adjective for windy is **breezy** (noun = **breeze**).

- When the weather is very cold it can be **icy** (noun = **ice**) or frosty. Ice is frozen water.

- We can also simply say that the weather is **good** or **bad**.

Clothes and seasons

- In cold weather people wear a **scarf** around their neck and **gloves** on their hands. Some people also wear a **hat** and a **jacket** or **coat**, especially if it's windy.

- In wet weather it's good to wear **boots** on your feet and to carry an **umbrella**; people can also wear a coat, especially one with a **hood** to cover their head.

- In hot weather people wear a hat, **sunglasses** for their eyes and put **suncream** or **sunscreen** on their body.

- Most countries have four seasons. In the UK/the US **spring** is quite warm, when the flowers appear; **summer** is hot; in [**autumn/fall**] it gets cool again and the trees lose their leaves, and **winter** is cold. Some (tropical) countries don't have four seasons, but they can have two – a **rainy** season, when it rains a lot, and a **dry** season, when it doesn't.

Questions and sentences

- We can use **Is it...?** with an adjective or a verb (the –ing form) to ask what the weather is like now:

Is it hot?	Yes, it is.
Is it raining?	No, it's stopped.

- We can also use **How + adjective + is it?** with adjectives like hot, cold, windy, etc., for example:

How windy is it?	Not too bad, now.
How icy is it?	It's very icy. Be careful when you drive to work today.

- If you want to ask for an item of clothing, use [**Have you got...?/Do you have...?**]

Have you got a hat?	Yes, why? Would you like to borrow it?

- We can use the question **What's the weather like?** to ask about the weather generally:

What's the weather like?	It's quite dull and windy.

- We can also ask this question with seasons or places.

What's the weather like in winter in your country?	It's cold, but it doesn't normally snow.

Practice

Exercise 1 In the word square there are four sets of three words linked by weather. In each set there is an adjective, a noun and a verb. Find all the words (twelve in total) then put them together in the correct sets and under the correct type of word (adjective, noun or verb).

D	Y	E	T	M	L	P	C	V	D	S	V
I	V	B	L	O	W	A	G	W	E	N	O
G	J	C	J	B	O	R	S	E	A	O	M
L	E	D	I	E	R	D	Y	T	T	W	O
O	B	U	C	N	A	V	C	U	B	E	K
V	R	T	Y	I	I	J	A	C	K	E	T
E	E	E	A	F	N	O	E	E	F	T	A
S	E	N	S	M	O	T	P	Z	P	B	E
E	Z	S	U	N	C	R	E	A	M	R	P
C	Y	I	I	E	R	E	L	H	J	I	T
O	A	G	S	H	I	N	E	O	M	G	R
P	J	E	R	A	J	W	J	P	W	H	U
U	M	B	R	E	L	L	A	E	Y	T	K
W	L	V	T	P	B	M	B	N	S	A	C

	adjective	noun	verb
Set 1	*breezy*	*jacket*	*blow*
Set 2			
Set 3			
Set 4			

Exercise 2 Look at these sentences and decide if they are right (✔) or wrong (✗), then correct those that are wrong.

1 It was so windy that my hat blew off. ✔
2 We never have rain at this time of year, it's normally very wet.
✗ We never have rain at this time of year, it's normally very dry.
3 It's very bright today, I need my sunglasses.
4 I don't like it when it's so humid – I want it to rain.
5 They say it will be very rain this afternoon.
6 There was still some snow on the road when I drove to work.
7 Hmm, it's quite dull outside. I think it might rain.
8 The weather was very warm so I put on a scarf.
9 Did you see the thunder last night?
10 Be careful driving today, it's quite ice outside.

Exercise 3 Complete the gaps in the following questions with one of the words in the box below. Be careful, *one* of the words isn't used.

1 Have you got an __umbrella__ ?	No, I haven't. But you can take this coat if you want.
2 How _____ is it?	It's boiling. Put some suncream on.
3 How _____ is it?	It's freezing. Put a scarf on.
4 How _____ is it?	It's quite bad. You'll need some boots.
5 Is it _____?	Yes, it is. I can hardly see anything outside.
6 What's the _____ like?	It's cold, but it's bright and sunny and quite frosty.
7 What's the weather like in _____ in your country?	Not bad. It's hot, but it's also very humid.

cold	dry	foggy	hot	wet	summer
	~~umbrella~~	weather			

Now check your answers.

▶ **Exercise 4 (Recordings 18.1, 18.2, 18.3, 18.4)** Pronunciation practice. Listen and repeat the words on the recording. Use the transcript at the back of the book to help you if necessary.

In use

Reading

Before you start, check you know these words:

> world   worse   extreme   flood   buildings
> transport   forest   fire   melt   cause   skin cancer   Earth

Note: The *North Pole* and the *South Pole* are at the top and bottom of the Earth – they are very cold places with lots of ice. *Strong* + noun means 'lots of' – strong wind means it's very windy.

Many people are worried about *global warming* – how the Earth is getting hotter and how dangerous that is. You are going to read part of the introduction to a book on global warming.

Reading 1 Read the passage. How much warmer could the Earth be by the year 2100?

> The world's weather is changing, and it's getting worse. Global warming does not mean it just gets hotter so that everyone at the North Pole goes out and buys suncream and sunglasses. It means the weather becomes more extreme. Let me show you what I mean.
>
> In the UK, the autumn of 2000 was the wettest autumn ever. There was a lot of rain and flooding and people's lives were ruined. Buildings and [transport/transportation] were also damaged by storms costing millions of pounds. In the US, strong winds blew forest fires almost out of control in California, putting people's lives in danger. At the North and South Poles, the temperature is becoming warmer, but this melts the ice and the sea rises. Some islands might disappear if this doesn't stop. In sunny Australia, the strong sun is a major cause of skin cancer. And I know we call it global *warming*, but it is also the reason why we sometimes get snow in summer which makes life impossible for our farmers.
>
> By the year 2100 the Earth could be six degrees warmer than it is now. That's crazy. It's time for it all to stop.

Reading 2 Read the passage again and answer the following questions.

1 What is becoming more extreme?   *the weather*
2 What was the autumn of 2000 like in the UK?

3 What kind of weather damaged buildings and [transport/transportation]?
4 What made forest fires worse in the US?
5 Are temperatures warmer or colder at the North and South Poles?
6 What is melting at the North and South Poles?
7 In Australia, what is a major cause of skin cancer?
8 What do we sometimes get in summer?

▶ Listening

Before you start, check you know these words:

> north   south   east   west   disappear   later
> temperature   finish

Note: *Slight* here means small, not much. A *shower* is a short period of rain. We give temperatures in *degrees centigrade (°C)* or *Fahrenheit (°F)* – at 0°C water becomes ice. When flowers are *in bloom* they open up and show their [colours/colors].

You are going to hear a weather forecast on the radio, it will describe what the weather will be like that day in Britain.

Listening 1 (Recording 18.5) Think how the weather is different in these four seasons – spring, summer, [autumn/fall] and winter. Now listen to the forecast and decide what season it is.

Listening 2 Listen to the recording again and complete the summary below by putting in the missing words.

> **South**
> A slight *frost* in the morning.
> Later on it will be _____.
>
> **North**
> Cold and _____ all day.
>
> **West**
> It will _____ in the morning.
> The afternoon should be quite _____.
>
> **East**
> It will be dry but _____.
> Temperatures will be 11 or _____ °C.
> _____ has finally finished!

Now check your answers.

Recap

Here are the words we learned in this unit. Do you know them all? Write down the translations if necessary.

Types of weather

sun	rain	wind
cloud	fog	snow
frost	storm	thunder
lightning	breeze	ice

Adjectives

sunny	rainy	windy
cloudy	foggy	snowy
frosty	wet	dry
humid	boiling	hot
warm	cool	cold
freezing	breezy	icy
bad	good	

Verbs

rain	snow	shine
blow		

Clothes and seasons

scarf	gloves	jacket
boots	umbrella	coat
hood	sunglasses	suncream, sunscreen
spring	summer	[autumn/fall]
winter	rainy season	dry season

Questions and sentences

Is it...?	How...is it?	What's the weather like (in...)?

What to do next

- Describe the weather today.
- Describe the weather in your country.
- Listen to a weather forecast or read one in the newspapers or on the Internet: how many words do you know?

Why not try this unit next?

- Clothes (1)

Answer key for this unit

Test your basics

		Noun	Adjective			Noun	Adjective
1		wind	windy	5		cloud	cloudy
2		storm	stormy	6		fog	foggy
3		rain	rainy	7		snow	snowy
4		sun	sunny				

Exercise 1

D	Y	E	T	M	L	P	C	V	D	S	V
I	V	B	L	O	W	A	G	W	E	N	O
G	J	C	J	B	O	R	S	E	A	O	M
L	E	D	I	E	R	D	Y	T	T	W	O
O	B	U	C	N	A	V	C	U	B	E	K
V	R	T	Y	I	I	J	A	C	K	E	T
E	E	E	A	F	N	O	E	E	F	T	A
S	E	N	S	M	O	T	P	Z	P	B	E
E	Z	S	U	N	C	R	E	A	M	R	P
C	Y	I	I	E	R	E	L	H	J	I	T
O	A	G	S	H	I	N	E	O	M	G	R
P	J	E	R	A	J	W	J	P	W	H	U
U	M	B	R	E	L	L	A	E	Y	T	K
W	L	V	T	P	B	M	B	N	S	A	C

	adjective	noun	verb
Set 1	breezy	jacket	blow
Set 2	bright	suncream	shine
Set 3	icy	gloves	snow
Set 4	wet	umbrella	rain

Exercise 2

1 It was so windy that my hat blew off. ✔
2 We never have rain at this time of year, it's normally very wet.
  ✗ We never have rain at this time of year, it's normally very
  dry.
3 It's very bright today, I need my sunglasses. ✔
4 I don't like it when it's so humid – I want it to rain. ✔
5 They say it will be very rain this afternoon. ✗ They say it
  will be very **rainy** this afternoon.
6 There was still some snow on the road when I drove to
  work. ✔

7 Hmm, it's quite dull outside. I think it might rain. ✔
8 The weather was very warm so I put on a scarf. ✗ The weather was very **cold** so I put on a scarf. (not cool).
9 Did you see the thunder last night? ✗ Did you see the **lightning** last night? *or* Did you **hear** the thunder last night?
10 Be careful driving today, it's quite ice outside. ✗ Be careful driving today, it's quite **icy** outside.

Exercise 3

1 Have you got an *umbrella*?
2 How *hot* is it?
3 How *cold* is it?
4 How *wet* is it?
5 Is it *foggy*?
6 What's the *weather* like?
7 What's the weather like in *summer* in your country?
(*dry* is not used.)

Reading

Reading 1 The Earth could be 6°C warmer by the year 2100.

Reading 2

1 The weather
2 Very wet (the wettest ever)
3 Storms
4 Strong winds
5 Warmer
6 The ice is melting
7 The strong sun
8 We sometimes get snow

Listening

Listening 1 It's spring (the weather is warmer, flowers are in bloom, winter has finally finished).

South
A slight *frost* in the morning.
Later on it will be *sunny*.

North
Cold and *cloudy* all day.

West
It will *rain* in the morning.
The afternoon should be quite *bright*.

East
It will be dry but *windy*.
Temperatures will be 11 or *12* °C.
Winter has finally finished!

transcripts

Note: For the listening exercises and dialogues we use these symbols to show whether the voice is American or British:

A = American   B = British.

Unit 1: Language to learn language

1.1 Types of word and grammar. Listen and repeat. Verb, adverb, noun, adjective, article, preposition, pronunciation, spelling, meaning, grammar, vocabulary, word order

1.2 Instructions. Listen and repeat. Question, exercise, answer, mark, fill the gap, correct, match, choose the correct answer, listen, repeat

1.3 Listening in class. Listen and repeat. Cassette, CD, recording, transcript, classwork, homework, check, teacher, student, whiteboard, blackboard, on your own, in pairs, group

1.4 Listening. Listen to this class and the instructions given.

B 1 **Teacher** OK, OK, good morning, everyone, good morning.
  Class Good morning.
  Teacher Right, we've got lots to do this morning, so let's get started. I think we'll start with last week's homework. I'm going to write up five mistakes from the homework on the whiteboard. I want you to work in pairs and see if you can correct the sentences. You have ten minutes.

B 2 **Student** Excuse me. Sorry, Steve?
  Teacher Yes?
  Student Could you tell me again what we have to do?

Teacher	Yes, certainly. You remember the vocabulary we just looked at?
Student	Yes?
Teacher	Well, we're using it in this exercise. You have to match the word on the left with it's meaning on the right, like in the example. Got that?
Student	Yes, I think so.
3 **Teacher**	...so are there any questions? No? All right, then, let's [practise/practice] the grammar with this little exercise, exercise 2. I want you to read each sentence, then choose the best answer, A, B, C or D. OK, got that? Good, you can start.
Student	What page was that?
Teacher	Sorry, that's page 32, grammar section, exercise 2.
Student	Thank you.
4 **Teacher**	OK, so let's move on to some listening. Do you remember what you have to do?
Class	Yes.
Teacher	Let's test you, Sandra. What do you have to do?
Sandra	We listen to the recording, and look at the sentences in our books, and we have to fill in the gaps with the missing word.
Teacher	Excellent. Right, everyone ready? Good, then let's start!

Unit 2: Ideas for learning language

2.1 Objects and sources. Listen and repeat. Dictionary, pen, notebook, cassette *or* tape recorder, cassette *or* tape, CD player, CD, song, television, [video recorder (video)/VCR], computer, CD-ROM, textbook, exercise, internet, books, magazines, newspapers

2.2 Verbs. Listen and repeat. Read, write, write down, record, listen, speak, ask, answer, search, look up, find out, do, [practise/practice]

2.3 Questions and answers. Listen and repeat these questions and answers from **Exercise 3**.

Have you got a dictionary?	Yes, I have.
May I borrow a pen?	No, I'm sorry, I'm using it.
May I use the computer?	Yes, of course.
Do you have a CD-ROM dictionary?	No, I don't.
May I listen to the radio?	No, I'm sorry, I need it myself.
May I read your magazine?	Yes, of course.

2.4 Listening. Listen to this interview with Marc, a student studying English, about his year in the USA.

A	**Interviewer**	Marc, you spent one year studying English in America. How was it?
A	**Marc**	Very hard at first. You hear the language all the time, and you get so tired. Or if you want to read a magazine, or a newspaper – again, it is in English. But it is good, the best way to learn.
	Interviewer	Why was it good being in America?
	Marc	Because you hear English all the time. You know, you watch television, and it's in English. You listen to the radio, and it's in English.
	Interviewer	Did you use your dictionary a lot?
	Marc	No, I didn't.
	Interviewer	No?
	Marc	No. I think looking in the dictionary all the time is a bad idea.
	Interviewer	Why?
	Marc	Well, if you're reading something, and you look in the dictionary for every word, it becomes boring and you don't want to read. And sometimes you forget. You look at every word, and at the end of the sentence you forget what it said!
	Interviewer	You stayed in New York. Did you know a lot about New York before you went?
	Marc	No, not much. But I looked up New York on the internet, you know, and all these pages came up. Of course, I couldn't read most of them, but I knew a few words, and there were pictures to help, so it was good.
	Interviewer	Marc, you're French. Was the English in New York different from that at school?
	Marc	Yes, well one thing I noticed, some spellings were different. And the pronunciation. You see we learned British English at school, and this was American English. So I wrote down both British and American English in my notebook. But they are not too different.
	Interviewer	Marc, thank you very much.

Unit 3: Animals

3.1 Animals and living places. Listen and repeat. Cat, dog, bird, horse, mouse (mice), elephant, cow, fish, lion, tiger, shark, snake, duck, sheep, camel, tortoise, nest, sea, river, lake

3.2 Parts of animals and verbs. Listen and repeat. Wings, beak, webbed feet, feathers, fin, tail, fur, skin, legs, paws, claws, teeth, hooves, fly, swim, run, crawl, scratch, bite

3.3 Adjectives. Listen and repeat. Big, small, fast, slow, dangerous, friendly, long, short, intelligent, stupid, sharp, soft, wild, tame

3.4 Descriptions. Listen to these sentences from **Exercise 3** in the book and repeat them.
1 The elephant is a large animal with four legs and [grey/gray] skin.
2 Be careful of the cat. She might scratch you with her claws.
3 I love sheep but they're so stupid. They always walk on the road in front of cars.
4 Our mouse is so soft. I love his [grey/gray] fur.
5 The lion comes from Africa; it is a very dangerous animal.

3.5 Listening. Listen to this quiz show on the radio called *Animal Rules* and do the exercises in the book.

Presenter Well, it's time for the last round here on *Animal Rules*. Jane, you're going to describe animals but you can't say the name. Rod, guess as many as you can in 60 seconds. OK, your time starts... now!

Jane Right. This animal is king of the jungle.

Rod Tiger?

Jane No! It's got brown fur, it lives in Africa, it's very dangerous.

Rod Lion.

Jane Yes! OK. This animal, um, it's also got brown fur, it's got four big paws... Um, it walks on two legs... Er... Paddington! Yes, Paddington...

Rod Bear?

Jane Correct! Now then. This animal is very small and it lives in water...

Rod Fish.

Jane Nearly. Lots of people have these as pets. Um... not silver but...

Rod Goldfish?

Jane That's it. OK, this animal is a bird but it doesn't live in nests in trees. It has webbed feet and it can swim.

Rod Must be a duck.

Jane Right! Now this animal. Small, very popular. Some people hate them but I love them. It has a tail, it drinks milk and eats birds.

Rod	Cat. I hate them.
Jane	Yes! Now this animal hates cats…
Presenter	Time's up!

Unit 4: Body (1)

4.1 Parts of the body. Listen and repeat. Head, face, eye, nose, hair, ear, cheek, lip, mouth, tooth (teeth)

4.2 Hair style. Listen and repeat. Long, short, straight, wavy, curly, bald, beard, moustache, clean-shaven

4.3 [Colours/colors] and qualities. Listen and repeat. Fair, dark, blond, brown, black, [grey/gray], white, red, green, blue, kind, friendly, unfriendly

4.4 Size, shape and age. Listen and repeat. Big, large, small, thick, thin, round, young, old

4.5 Listen and repeat the corrected sentences from **Exercise 3**.
1 What [colour/color] are your eyes?
2 My father's hair is very [grey/gray].
3 I don't like my ears; they're too big.
4 I have quite a big head.
5 What is her face like?
6 She's got a nice face, big blue eyes, and long dark hair.
7 Steve has a moustache and a beard.
8 I don't like beards; I'm clean-shaven.

4.6 Listening. What's in a face? Listen to this radio [programme/program].

B **Jenny**	OK, I'm talking to Mike. Whose picture do you have, Mike?
B **Mike**	It's a picture of my father, taken twenty years ago.
Jenny	Right, and what's your father like?
Mike	Well, his hair was still brown then – it's [grey/gray] now, of course – and it's also quite long, which is very funny.
Jenny	Why's it funny?
Mike	Because he hates long hair on men now! He's always telling me to get my hair cut.
Jenny	No!
Mike	Yeah! Um, he has quite a thin face, quite a good-looking face, I think too. My mother always found him good-looking.

Jenny	I hope so! So is there anything he doesn't like about his face.
Mike	Well, his nose. He's always hated his nose. He thinks it's too big. My mother used to make jokes about it when she was angry with him.
Jenny	OK. Anything else?
Mike	Yes, his ears. He thinks they're too small!
Jenny	All right, what does he like about his face?
Mike	His eyes. Definitely. He has big blue eyes. He says every woman loves them!
Jenny	What does your mother say to that, then?
Mike	She has to agree, says it's why she married him.
Jenny	OK, and why do you like this picture?
Mike	I like this picture because you see what my father is really like. You see a really kind face. He looks so happy, you know, standing there with my mother, with this wonderful smile, and I just like looking at it, because, you know, I think that's my dad, and he's such a nice guy.

Unit 5: Body (2)

5.1 Parts of the body. Listen and repeat. Leg, arm, hand, stomach, knee, finger, elbow, ankle, foot (feet), toe

5.2 Adjectives. Listen and repeat. Tall, short, fair-skinned, dark-skinned, black, white, Asian, good-looking, beautiful, handsome, overweight, slim, well-built, thin, fat, big, small, long, short

5.3 Size. Listen and repeat. Weight, height, pound, kilogram, foot (feet), inch, [centimetre/centimeter]

5.4 Questions and answers. Listen and repeat these questions and answers taken from **Exercises 2** and **3**.

What does Tim look like?	He's tall, well-built and has short, dark, straight hair and big green eyes.
How heavy is Jenny?	She weighs 88 pounds.
What [colour/color] is Tim's hair?	It's dark.
What does Jenny look like?	She's quite short, quite good-looking, and she's got long, blond, curly hair and blue eyes.
How tall is Tim?	He's six feet tall.

What is Jenny's hair like?	It's long, blond, and curly.
What [colour/color] are Jenny's eyes?	They're blue.
What does Tim weigh?	He weighs 220 pounds.

5.5 Listening. Listen to the description of three robbers on 'Police – Help!'

B Presenter   …all the news we have. Well now, let's turn to our next case, this one, a rather nasty robbery in the village of Borham, in Sussex. Constable Fiona Garrond of Sussex Constabulary is here to describe the men. Fiona?

B Fiona   Yes, thank you. The police are looking for three men and have given a description. The first man is six feet tall, and he weighs about 200 pounds. He has long dark hair and blue eyes. He was wearing a pair of dirty jeans and a brown sweater.

Presenter   Right, so that's six feet tall, weight 200 pounds, long, dark hair, and blue eyes. Good. And the second man?

Fiona   The second man is smaller. He is 5 feet 6 inches tall and is described as well-built. Witnesses say he weighs about 250 pounds. His eyes are brown, and he has short, [grey/gray] hair. He has a beard. He was wearing a pair of jeans and a black T-shirt.

Presenter   OK. 5 feet 6, 250 pounds, blue eyes, and short [grey/gray] hair. And the last man?

Fiona   Yes. Now, the last man is the most dangerous. He's quite tall, about 5 feet 10, and he weighs 200 pounds. He's clean-shaven, and has very short red hair. What people really notice are his eyes – he has large eyes that are very blue. He's wearing dark trousers and a shirt, and he's carrying a gun, so please take care if you see him.

Presenter   5 feet 10, 200 pounds, um, short red hair, and blue eyes. Right. So, what happened?

Fiona   Well, it was on 7th March last year at around 6 o'clock…

Unit 6: Clothes (1)

6.1 Clothes for the legs and feet. Listen and repeat. Shoes, boots, [trousers/pants], jeans, shorts, skirt, [trainers/sneakers], socks, [underpants/shorts], [knickers/panties], [tights/pantyhose]

6.2 Clothing for the rest of the body. Listen and repeat. Sweater, T-shirt, shirt, jacket, coat, dress, hat, blouse, tie, suit, [trouser suit/pantsuit], [vest/undershirt], bra, pyjamas, nightdress, nightgown

6.3 Extras and make-up. Listen and repeat. Belt, [handbag/purse], earrings, necklace, bracelet, ring, lipstick, mascara, eye shadow

6.4 Verbs and singular and plural. Listen and repeat. Wear, get dressed, get undressed, put on, take off, change, a, an, pair of, a skirt, a jacket, a pair of jeans, a pair of boots

6.5 Listen and repeat these sentences from **Exercise 3**.

What do you wear at the weekend?	I normally wear a pair of jeans.
It's hot! Can I take my sweater off?	Of course.
What's Mike wearing today?	His new suit. Horrible, isn't it!
Do you like my [trousers/pants]?	Yes, I really like them.
What did you buy yesterday?	A pair of shoes. Do you like them?
Are you all right?	No, I think I need a belt for these [trousers/pants].
Where's Sue?	She's putting on her lipstick. She won't be a minute.
What's the first thing you do when you come home from work?	Easy. I change my clothes.
What's the American word for tights?	Pantyhose.
What do you think of my dress?	Sorry, I don't like it much.

6.6 Listening. Listen to a woman telling her husband about her shopping trip.

Tim Lucy, is that you?
Lucy Yes. Phew! Back at last. I'm exhausted.
Tim I'm not surprised! What have you bought? Is there anything left in the stores?
Lucy I've not bought much at all. I just needed a few things. Do you want to see what?

Tim	Go on. I don't think I have a choice.
Lucy	Well, I need some more things for work, so I bought these two skirts. What do you think, do you like them?
Tim	Yes, yes they're nice. OK, what else?
Lucy	There was a sale on at Lady D's, and they had this great pair of pants. I've been looking at them for a long time, but the price was good, so I bought them. Here you are, what do you think?
Tim	Yes, they're nice too.
Lucy	And I also got this blouse to go with it. Well, actually, I bought three blouses.
Tim	Three?
Lucy	Yes, well, I couldn't decide which one to get, so I got all three. I knew you wouldn't mind.
Tim	Hmm.
Lucy	And then I saw there was a new shoe store in town, so I just went in for a quick look, and, Tim, you're going to love these. I got this great pair of boots. Look, aren't they great?
Tim	Yes, they're really nice… So, did you bring back anything for me?
Lucy	Of course I did.
Tim	Really? What?
Lucy	Well, it's winter soon, so I got you two sweaters. And, of course, the credit card bill, you can have that too.
Tim	Great.

Unit 7: Clothes (2)

7.1 Shops, departments, types of clothes, and extras. Listen and repeat. [Clothes shop/clothing store], [shoe shop/shoe store], department store, changing room, dry cleaner's, lingerie, accessories, [jewellery/jewelry], cosmetics

7.2 Length, size, and tightness. Listen and repeat. Long, short, big, small, tight, loose

7.3 Materials and pattern. Listen and repeat. Denim, wool, cotton, linen, leather, silk, striped, flowery, [spots/polka dots]

7.4 General. Listen and repeat. Fashionable, unfashionable, smart, scruffy, casual, comfortable, uncomfortable, great, beautiful, new, old

7.5 Listen and repeat these questions, sentences and replies from **Exercise 3**.

How do I look in these jeans?	Oh, they really suit you.
What do you think of my new coat?	I really like it. How much was it?
What's your new dress like?	It's blue and white striped and made of cotton.
I'm looking for some smart trousers.	Certainly. I have a nice pair here.
I'd like a new suit.	Of course. And do you need a tie to go with it?
Can I try these trousers on?	Certainly. The changing room is just over here.
How much is this jacket?	£60. Would you like to try it on?

7.6 Listening. Listen to the three short conversations.

1 Shop assistant Good morning, Madam, can I help you?

Sally Yes, I'm looking for a smart suit for work.

Shop assistant Certainly, Madam, always very useful. We have some just over here... Now, if you're looking for a trouser suit, this is a very nice suit. It's made from linen, which should keep you nice and cool.

Sally Yes, it looks nice. I might try it on, thank you. Oh, and can you just tell me how much this sweater is?

Shop assistant Sorry, which one, Madam?

Sally This green sweater over here.

Shop assistant Ah, yes, that's £15 at the moment. We've got a sale on.

Sally Excellent. I think I might get that then. Thanks very much.

Shop assistant You're welcome.

2 Sally I'd like to see that pair of brown leather boots you have in the window.

Shop assistant Of course... Here you are.

Sally Hmm, yes, they're very nice.

Shop assistant Would you like to try them on?

Sally Yes, please.

Shop assistant Oh, they look really nice, they really suit you.

Sally Do you think so?

Shop assistant Oh, yes, really nice.

Sally Hmm. How much are they?

Shop assistant Two hundred and fifty pounds.

Sally Two hundred and fifty pounds! Hmm, maybe not today, thanks.

3 **Sally** Well, what do you think of my new dress?

Tony Oh yes, it looks really nice. What's it made of?

Sally It's wool. It's quite tight. I'm really pleased with it. Do you want to see what else I've bought?

Tony Sure.

Sally Well, I got a pair of black jeans, because my other jeans are getting rather old.

Tony Right. Yes. Nice. Anything else?

Sally Well, I nearly got this beautiful pair of brown leather boots, but they were two hundred and fifty pounds...

Tony Two hundred and fifty pounds!

Sally Exactly. So, for a change, I got a pair of trainers instead. They were only sixty pounds.

Tony Great.

Unit 8: Drinks

8.1 Hot and cold drinks. Listen and repeat. Tea, coffee, hot chocolate, sugar, lemon, cream, water, milk, orange juice, lemonade, tonic, Coca-Cola, pineapple juice, grapefruit juice, apple juice, ice

8.2 Alcoholic drinks. Listen and repeat. Beer, wine, spirits, bitter, lager, [whisky/whiskey], brandy, vodka, gin

8.3 Places to drink and amounts. Listen and repeat. Restaurant, [café/coffee shop], pub, bar, glass, cup, pot, pint, half a pint, [litre/liter], half a [litre/liter], bottle

8.4 Adjectives. Listen and repeat. [Fizzy/carbonated], still, soft, black coffee, white coffee, red wine, white wine

8.5 Listen and repeat these phrases from **Exercise 3**.

What would you like?	I'd like an orange juice, please.
Are you thirsty?	Yes, I am. Have you got anything to drink?
I'm thirsty.	OK, what can I get you?
I'd like a coffee, please.	Certainly. Would you like it black or with cream?
Would you like a glass of water?	Oh yes, please. I'm very thirsty.
Would you prefer tea or coffee?	Coffee, please.
Could I have a glass of lemonade, please?	Of course. Would you like ice with that?
What can I get you?	A glass of red wine, please.

8.6 Listening. Listen to these conversations.

1
Sam	Laura, it's so good to see you! Come in, come in, you must be freezing!
Laura	Thanks! Yes, I am cold.
Sam	Let's get that wet coat off. Would you like something to drink?
Laura	Oh yes, something hot if you're making it.
Sam	Of course. Tea? Coffee?
Laura	Coffee, please.
Sam	No problem. Um, how do you take it? White? Black?
Laura	White please. With two sugars.
Sam	White with two sugars coming up!

2
Waiter	Would you like anything to go with your meal?
Customer	Yes, I think we'd like a bottle of wine, please.
Waiter	Red or white, sir?
Customer	Well, as we're both having the beef, I think it has to be red.
Waiter	Then may I suggest this Bordeaux, sir?
Customer	Hmm, yes, that looks nice. I think we'll take it.
Waiter	Thank you, sir.

3
Waitress	Can I help you?
Customer	Yes, I think we'll have two slices of that chocolate cake.
Waitress	Certainly. And what would you like to drink?
Customer	A pot of tea, please.
Waitress	Two slices of chocolate cake... and a pot of tea... Right. Anything else?
Customer	Yes, could we have two glasses of water as well, please?
Waitress	Of course, no problem. That'll be $8 all together, please.
Customer	Thank you.

4
Landlady	Good evening, gents. What can I get you?
Customer	Right, I'd like two pints of lager.
Landlady	Two pints of lager... Right. Anything else?
Customer	Yes, a pint of bitter.
Landlady	A pint of bitter... OK, anything else?
Customer	Yes. Just a glass of lemonade, please. I'm driving.
Landlady	Would you like ice in that?
Customer	Um... yes, yes I would, thanks.

Unit 9: Family

9.1 Family. Listen and repeat. Dad, father, [mum/mom], mother, son, daughter, brother, sister, grandfather, grandmother, grandson, granddaughter, uncle, aunt, cousin, nephew, niece

9.2 More family. Listen and repeat. Wife, husband, parents, brother-in-law, sister-in-law, half-sister, stepmother, relation

9.3 Marriage. Listen and repeat. Be married, get married, married, widowed, widower, widow, divorced, single, ex-husband

9.4 Listen and repeat these phrases from **Exercise 3**.

Have you got any cousins?	Yes I have. I have two cousins.
Is your sister older than you?	No, she isn't. She's two years younger.
How many brothers and sisters have you got?	I've got one brother and one sister.
Are you married?	No, I'm not. I'm single.
Do you like your brother?	No, I don't really like him, although I do like my sister.
Who's your [favourite/favorite] relation?	My Aunt Polly. She's great. She's so much fun.

9.5 Listening. Listen to this interview.

A Salesman Right, now, family. I need you to answer some questions. First, are you married?

B Woman No, I'm not.

Salesman Right... are you widowed, divorced?

Woman No, I'm single. I've never been married.

Salesman Never...been...married... OK. Have you got any children?

Woman No, I haven't.

Salesman Good. No children. Right. Have you got any brothers or sisters?

Woman Does that include stepbrothers and stepsisters?

Salesman No, only those that are related by blood. That includes half-brothers and sisters, but not step-relations or in-laws.

Woman OK, well I have two sisters, and one brother. That should be one half-brother.

Salesman So that's two sisters...

Woman Yes.

Salesman And one half-brother. Good. Oh, I missed the most important one of all! What about your parents, are they still alive?

Woman Well, my mother is, but she's a widow. I also have a stepfather. Is that important?

Salesman   No, just your real mother and father, thanks. Right, next section. Work. Do you...

Unit 10: Food (1)

10.1 Types of food. Listen and repeat. Fruit, vegetable, meat, dairy, snack, [sweets/candy]

10.2 Fruit, vegetables and meat. Listen and repeat. Orange, apple, banana, pear, lemon, onion, potato, peas, carrot, salad, fish, chicken, beef, lamb, pork, steak

10.3 Dairy and snacks. Listen and repeat. Milk, butter, cheese, egg, yoghurt, sandwich, [crisps/potato chips], [chips/French fries], chocolate

10.4 Meals. Listen and repeat. Have a meal, breakfast, lunch, dinner, supper, toast, jam, marmalade, cereal, soup, rice, pasta, sugar, flour, salt, pepper

10.5 Listen and repeat these sentences from **Exercise 3**.

What time do you have breakfast?	Quite late, at eight o'clock.
Do you like chicken?	No, I don't. I don't like any meat.
What would you like to eat for lunch?	Could I have some soup, please?
Would you like something to eat?	No, thanks. I'm not hungry at the moment.
I'm hungry.	OK, would you like a sandwich?
Could I have some fruit, please?	Of course. Would you like an apple, a pear, or an orange?
Are you hungry?	No, I'm not. How about you?
I'd like a sandwich, please.	OK, what would you like in it? Cheese? Jam?

10.6 Listening. Listen to these three short conversations.

1	**Man**	Jenny?
	Woman	Yes?
	Man	Do you like beef?
	Woman	Yes, I do. Why?

	Man	I want to invite you to dinner on Saturday. We're having roast beef, um, roast potatoes, everything.
	Woman	Oh, that's very kind. What time?
	Man	Half past seven.
	Woman	Yes, that should be fine. Thanks.
B 2	**Woman**	Excuse me, sir. We're doing a survey on eating habits. Would you mind answering a few questions?
B	**Man**	No, not at all.
	Woman	Thank you. OK, could you tell me, do you have breakfast?
	Man	Yes, I do.
	Woman	OK. What do you have for breakfast?
	Man	I normally have toast, with jam or marmalade.
	Woman	Right. Now lunch. What do you have for lunch?
	Man	Ah, well, I only have a short time so...
A 3	**Son**	Mom, I'm hungry.
A	**Mother**	Well, it's dinner soon.
	Son	But I'm hungry now.
	Mother	Well, what would you like?
	Son	Could I have a sandwich?
	Mother	No. You can have some potato chips if you like, but nothing else.
	Son	Oh, all right then.

Unit 11: Food (2)

11.1 Equipment. Listen and repeat. Oven, [grill/broiler], hob, saucepan, frying pan, microwave, [jug/pitcher], knife, fork, spoon, [scales/measuring cups]

11.2 Preparing food. Listen and repeat. Measure, pour, mix, stir, cut, chop, beat, add, serve, [litre/liter], pint, kilogram, pound

11.3 Ways of cooking. Listen and repeat. Oil, fat, fry (fried), boil (boiled), simmer, [grill (grilled)/broil (broiled)], bake (baked), roast (roast), raw, freeze (frozen)

11.4 Nouns and adjectives. Listen and repeat. Ingredients, recipe, curry, hot, cold, spicy, mild, sweet, sour, bitter, [savoury/savory], salty, delicious, tasteless, tasty

11.5 Listen and repeat these sentences from **Exercise 2**.

B	**Waiter**	Good evening, sir. Good evening, madam. Are you ready to order?

Woman	Yes we are, please.
Waiter	What would you like, madam?
Woman	I'd like the steak, please.
Waiter	Steak. Certainly. And for you, sir?
Man	I'd like the chicken, please.
Waiter	Yes, sir.
Woman	And could we have a bottle of wine, please?
Waiter	Of course, madam. Red or white?

11.6 Listening. Listen to this recipe from a radio show.

1 Here's today's quick recipe. First the ingredients. You need four slices of white bread, some butter, some raisins, 120g of sugar – that's two ounces for those older listeners. Also two eggs and half a pint of milk, that is a quarter of a [litre/liter], and a little vanilla extract. Right, we're ready to begin.

2 Now, the first thing you do is to spread the butter on the bread. Be generous. Then make two sandwiches from the bread. Cut each sandwich into about six pieces. Next put the bread into a dish and then add the raisins and sugar. Put the eggs into a bowl and beat them and stir in the milk and vanilla extract. Then pour the mixture over the bread. Leave for 15 minutes, then put in a hot oven, 190°C, that's 400°F, for 35–40 minutes. Finally serve hot with cream.

Unit 12: House and household (1)

12.1 Parts of a house. Listen and repeat. House, roof, garden, garage, gate, [flat/apartment], front door, hedge, fence, window, wall, household

12.2 Rooms. Listen and repeat. Room, floor, upstairs, downstairs, kitchen, dining room, living room, hall, toilet, basement, cellar, bedroom, bathroom, study, attic, loft, [front or back garden/front or backyard], lawn, patio, driveway, flowers, trees

12.3 Adjectives. Listen and repeat. Household, big, large, small, bright, dark, warm, cold, old, new, traditional, modern, beautiful, ugly

12.4 Listen and repeat these sentences from **Exercise 2**.

How many rooms has your house got?

It's got six rooms – a kitchen, a living room, a bathroom, and three bedrooms.

What's your garden like?	It's beautiful, with lots of flowers and a big lawn.
Where do you live?	We live in a modern apartment.
What's your bedroom like?	Our bedroom is only small, but it's really warm in winter.
Does your house have a backyard?	Yes it has. It has a big garden with a small patio.
What [colour/color] is your bathroom?	Our bathroom is blue.
What's your house like?	It's quite old. It's got a small front garden; it hasn't got a garage, but it has a driveway and it has three bedrooms.

12.5 Listening. Listen to Steve and Cath deciding which house to buy.

A Cath Well, what did you think? I think it's clear the last house, Morley Road, was the best.

A Steve Hmm, yes, maybe, but it's also the most expensive. And it's a really ugly house, too.

Cath Yes, but it has four bedrooms. Even though one of them is that horrible green [colour/color].

Steve All right, well let's think about the others. What about Clifton Court? It's a lot cheaper, and it had that great big living room, really bright and airy. And the bedrooms were really warm, great for winter.

Cath Yes, but no garden. Imagine our three children without a garden. We'd go crazy.

Steve What about Mandarin Gardens?

Cath Well, I liked it. The garage was rather old, but that's not too important. And the garden was beautiful. It was definitely my [favourite/favorite] garden.

Steve Yes, and the rooms were big too. I like modern houses, though the windows were quite small, I didn't like that. Still the price is good.

Cath True... But it still only has three bedrooms. We need four bedrooms. I think we should buy Morley Road.

Steve Well, I have to agree. Morley Road it is then. I'll go and phone the realtor.

Unit 13: House and household (2)

13.1 Furniture and furnishings in the living room. Listen and repeat. Table, chair, sofa, armchair, carpet, curtains, light, lamp, TV, [video/VCR], hi-fi, fire, picture, plant, vase

13.2 In the kitchen. Listen and repeat. Cupboard, sink, fridge, freezer, [cooker/stove], washing machine, dishwasher, plate, bowl, cup, glass, knife, fork, spoon

13.3 In the bathroom and bedroom. Listen and repeat. Bath, shower, [basin/sink], towel, toilet, [wardrobe/closet], chest of drawers, bedside cabinet, bedside table, bed, mirror, sheet, pillow, blanket, quilt

13.4 Adjectives and prepositions. Listen and repeat. Comfortable, uncomfortable, heavy, light, next to, between, on the right, behind, in front of, under, on top of, opposite, near

13.5 Listen and repeat these questions and sentences from **Exercise 3**.

Where's the hi-fi?	It's on the chest of drawers behind the sofa.
Have you got a television?	Yes, we have. And we've got a VCR too.
What's in this cupboard?	Oh, just some plates, bowls, knives, forks, and spoons.
What's your living room like?	It's quite big. We've got two armchairs and a great, big comfortable sofa to sit on.

13.6 Listening. Listen to Jenny and Pete as they try to arrange their bedroom.

Pete Before we start moving any furniture, let's think about what goes where.

Jenny I agree. Well, the bed. That's first. It's so big I think we have to put it opposite the window, near the door.

Pete OK. And let's put the wardrobe next to the bed.

Jenny What, next to the door?

Pete No, not next to the door, on the other side, on the right-hand side, against the wall.

Jenny Umm, all right then, I suppose it's nice and near for the clothes. So the bedside cabinet goes on the other side of the bed, right? On the left-hand side.

Pete	Yes, that's right. I know it's near the door, but it's only small. The door will still open.
Jenny	OK. Then the table. The table we can put in the far corner, next to the window and opposite the wardrobe.
Pete	Why that side?
Jenny	Because there's a socket there, and we can put the spare TV on the table and watch TV in bed.
Pete	OK…
Jenny	And the chair goes in the left corner, which just leaves the chest of drawers, which… which goes between the chair and the TV.
Pete	What, under the window?
Jenny	Yes, under the window. What do you think?
Pete	Hmm… yeah, OK, that sounds good. Why not?

Unit 14: People and jobs

14.1 People and jobs. Listen and repeat. Police officer, policeman, policewoman, lawyer, doctor, nurse, teacher, student, engineer, businessman, businesswoman, secretary, civil servant, farmer, housewife, househusband, worker, colleague, manager, boss

14.2 Types of work. Listen and repeat. Company, government, profession, professional, law, education, medicine, IT, study, qualified, training

14.3 Places and conditions. Listen and repeat. Office, factory, farm, hospital, [surgery/doctor's office], school, at home, earn, get paid, [holiday/vacation]

14.4 Describing jobs and colleagues. Listen and repeat. Wonderful, awful, friendly, unfriendly, interesting, boring, generous, mean, strict, easy-going, polite, rude, shy, self-confident, helpful, unhelpful, sensitive, insensitive

14.5 Listen and repeat these sentences and questions from **Exercise 2.**

Who do you work for?	I work for Juice Computers.
Where do you work?	I work in a factory in California.
What do you do?	I'm a computer engineer.
When do you work?	I work from 8a.m. until 6p.m.
How much vacation do you get a year?	I get 4 weeks' vacation a year.

How much do you get paid? I get $50,000 a year.
What are your colleagues   Really friendly and
  like?   easy-going.

14.6 Listening. Listen to this extract of *Everyone but the Busman* on the radio.

Fiona	Hello, it's Tom, isn't it? I'm Fiona.
Tom	Oh, hi.
Fiona	What are you doing?
Tom	Oh, just thinking. About the others.
Fiona	Yes, me too. So then, what do you think?
Tom	Oh, well, let me see. Eric seems really friendly and easy-going, I like him. And he's an engineer too, which will be really useful. And you seem very friendly.
Fiona	I have to be. It's my job.
Tom	Really? What do you do?
Fiona	I'm a nurse. What do you think of Liz?
Tom	She seems incredibly self-confident, doesn't she? I can't believe she's a housewife. She should be a police officer or something.
Fiona	Yes, that's true. She seems OK, but I tell you what, that businesswoman, I don't like her.
Tom	What, Stella? Yeah, I'm not sure about her.
Fiona	Talk about being mean – she didn't even buy a round of drinks. I don't know why she came – we won't be making any money on that island.
Tom	I totally agree!

Unit 15: Shopping

15.1 In a shop. Listen and repeat. [Shop assistant/salesperson], manager, customer, basket, [trolley/shopping cart], shopping bag, price, cash register, checkout, [queue/line], aisle

15.2 Common shops and stores. Listen and repeat. Bank, [chemist/ pharmacy], [newsagent/news stand], [off-licence/ liquor store], supermarket, post office, [petrol station/gas station], travel agent's, [estate agent's/realtor]

15.3 Measures and numbers. Listen and repeat. [Litre/liter], pint, kilo, pound, a quarter, a half, three-quarters, box, tube, [packet/package]

15.4 Verbs. Present and past tense. Listen and repeat. Sell, sold, buy, bought, pay, paid, cost, cost

15.5 Listen and repeat these sentences taken from **Exercise 3**.

Can I help you?	Yes, I'd like some milk, please.
Certainly, sir. How much would you like?	Two [litres/liters].
Right then, two [litres/liters]. Anything else?	Yes, have you got any cheese?
Of course, sir. How much cheese would you like?	Half a pound, please. Do you sell newspapers?
I'm sorry, I'm afraid we don't.	Oh well, never mind. How much is that?
£7.63 please, sir.	Here you are.
Thank you, sir. Here's your change.	Thank you, goodbye.
Goodbye.	

15.6 Listening. Listen to this telephone conversation between a customer, and the telephone shopping service from the supermarket Coset.

B Operator	Hello, Coset Home Shopping Service.
B Mrs. Jones	Hello, I'd like to make an order.
Operator	Could I have your membership number, please?
Mrs. Jones	Yes, it's WF 297, Mrs. Jones.
Operator	Thank you Mrs. Jones. Can I have your order, please?
Mrs. Jones	Can I have three pounds of minced beef?
Operator	Yes…
Mrs. Jones	Then two bottles of white wine… um… Chardonnay, please.
Operator	OK. Anything else?
Mrs. Jones	Three loaves of French bread.
Operator	Three loaves… right. Is that all?
Mrs. Jones	Do you have any strawberries?
Operator	I'm afraid not. We do have some excellent peaches though.
Mrs. Jones	OK, I'll have some of those.
Operator	How many would you like?
Mrs. Jones	Um… 12 should be enough. And that's it. How much is that?
Operator	It's £13.37, to be added to your monthly bill.
Mrs. Jones	When will it be delivered?
Operator	This afternoon.
Mrs. Jones	That's great. Thank you. Goodbye.
Operator	Goodbye, madam.

Unit 16: Time (1)

16.1 Nouns. Listen and repeat. Day, week, weekdays, weekend, month, year, leap year, date, calendar, diary

16.2 Days and months. Listen and repeat. Monday, Tuesday, Wednesday, Thursday, Friday, Saturday, Sunday, January, February, March, April, May, June, July, August, September, October, November, December

16.3 Dates and years. Listen and repeat. Nineteen hundred, nineteen ninety-nine, two thousand, two thousand and eleven, the first of January, January the first

16.4 Seasons and special dates. Listen and repeat. Winter, spring, summer, [autumn/fall], Christmas, Christmas Day, Easter, public holiday, bank holiday, birthday

16.5 Listen and repeat these sentences from **Exercise 3**.
Why don't you come around on Saturday?
What day is it? It's Friday.
Our daughter was born in the year two thousand.
When's your birthday? On 6th April.
I'm seeing the doctor on Wednesday.
Are you free on Tuesday? I'll look in my diary and check.
We always visit our grandparents at Easter.
This winter was really cold.
What day is your birthday this year? It's on Sunday.
I hate February. It's a horrible month.

16.6 Listening. *Times of My Life* is a radio show where a celebrity is interviewed about his or her life. Listen to this introduction.

Welcome once again to *Times of My Life*. This week, we have an actress. She was born on May the fourth, 1962, the daughter of famous actor Michael Warren. Do you know who it is? She was married in 1988, and had a son, also called Michael, who was born on Christmas Day, 1992. She became an actress later in life and didn't make her first movie until 1990. Tragically, her father never saw it, because Michael Warren died in 1986, but critics immediately said she had his talent. She nearly died in a serious car crash in March 1997, and was in hospital for a year. But last year she starred in the great smash hit, *Conflict of the Galaxies*, as Lady Dread, and next month we will see the release of *Conflict of the Galaxies II*. I am of course talking about Amanda Warren, and here she is. Amanda Warren!

Unit 17: Time (2)

17.1 Time. Listen and repeat. The time, hour, minute, second, o'clock, past, to, a quarter, half, five past two, half past two, a quarter to three, two twenty, a.m., p.m., morning, noon, afternoon, evening, night, watch, clock

17.2 More days. Listen and repeat. Today, yesterday, the day before yesterday, tomorrow, the day after tomorrow, last week, next Christmas, two months ago, in three days' time

17.3 Modifiers, nouns and verbs. Listen and repeat. On time, early, late, take, long, short, meeting, [holiday/vacation], wait

17.4 Listen and repeat these sentences from **Exercise 3**.

What time is it?	About half past three.
How long is your meeting?	About fifty minutes. I'll meet you for lunch afterwards.
What time do you get up?	I normally get up at a quarter past seven.
What time is your meeting?	About 10:50. I'll meet you for lunch afterwards.
How long does it take to go to work?	It normally takes me about twenty-five minutes.

17.5 Listening. Listen to Bob ask Fiona about her holiday plans.

Bob You're off on your holidays, aren't you?

Fiona That's right, we're off to sunny Greece.

Bob When are you going?

Fiona We're off tomorrow.

Bob Do you want a lift to the airport?

Fiona No, thanks, we're getting a taxi.

Bob Right. What time is the taxi coming?

Fiona Half past six in the morning. It's going to be horrible. Last time the taxi was late, though, and we nearly missed our plane.

Bob When are you coming back?

Fiona We're coming back in two weeks' time. I'm not looking forward to the flight, though. I hate flying.

Bob How long is the flight?

Fiona Four hours. It's not too bad. And then it's only a short ride to our hotel. We should be there by four thirty local time and out in the sun. I can't wait.

Bob I'll bet. Lucky you!

Unit 18: Weather

18.1 Types of weather. Listen and repeat. Sun, rain, wind, cloud, fog, snow, frost, storm, thunder, lightning, breeze, ice

18.2 Adjectives and verbs. Listen and repeat. Sunny, rainy, windy, cloudy, foggy, snowy, frosty, wet, dry, humid, boiling, hot, warm, cool, cold, freezing, breezy, icy, good, bad, rain, snow, shine, blow

18.3 Clothes. Listen and repeat. Scarf, gloves, jacket, boots, umbrella, coat, hood, sunglasses, suncream, sunscreen, spring, summer, [autumn/fall], winter, rainy season, dry season

18.4 Listen and repeat these sentences from **Exercise 3**.

Have you got an umbrella?	No, I haven't. But you can take this coat if you want.
How hot is it?	It's boiling. Put some suncream on.
How cold is it?	It's freezing. Put a scarf on.
How wet is it?	It's quite bad. You'll need some boots.
Is it foggy?	Yes, it is. I can hardly see anything outside.
What's the weather like?	It's cold, but it's bright and sunny and quite frosty.
What's the weather like in summer in your country?	Not bad. It's hot, but it's also very humid.

18.5 Listening. Listen to this weather forecast.

Newsreader Well, it's 6:25 and here's Sarah with the weather. Sarah.

Sarah Yes, thank you. Well, today will be a much better day than yesterday. Here in the south, we might start with a slight frost in the morning, but that will disappear and it should become sunny later on. Not so good up in the north, I'm afraid, where it's going to be cold and cloudy, with a chance of showers all day. In the west too it will rain in the morning, but it will clear up and the afternoon should be quite bright. The east will stay dry, but it will be very windy I'm afraid. Temperatures will be quite warm in the afternoon, about 11 or 12 degrees centigrade, that's 60 degrees Fahrenheit, so we might get the first flowers of the year in bloom, and I think we can say that winter has finally finished.

Newsreader Sarah, that's excellent news. I'll put away my scarf and gloves. Thank you. And the headlines again. A 30-year-old man has been jailed for...

Reading exercises

The following Reading texts have been recorded for extra listening practice: Unit 2, Unit 3, Unit 4, Unit 5, Unit 6, Unit 9, Unit 10, Unit 11, Unit 13, Unit 14, Unit 17 and Unit 18.